Jesus and the Church

THE CATHOLIC FAITH SERIES

Volume One

Libreria Editrice Vaticana

United States Conference of Catholic Bishops
Washington, DC

Preface

How did the project for this book come about?

For about three years, I have been placing in the Basilica of San Carlo al Corso (Rome), of which I am rector, some catechetical pamphlets on topics related to current events, available to anyone who comes into the basilica. And to my surprise I noticed that more than 2.5 million pamphlets have been taken by people passing through the basilica. So in response to the demand from so many people, I decided to collect, in a compact and portable format, the pamphlets in question.

What criterion was used to select the topics?

The criterion of relevance. I decided to present brief summaries of what the Catholic Church teaches about some of the timely topics that are being brought to people's attention now for various reasons. In some cases I have also tried to select topics that are somewhat forgotten by many Christians today, or even disputed by some of them.

Illustration: © *Fotosearch.com*

ISBN 978-1-60137-337-3

First printing, December 2012

Contents

What documents were used in addressing these topics?

Mainly the documents of the Holy See, and for two reasons. First, because these documents tend to be overlooked by the general public, and their richness, comprehensiveness, and beauty deserve to be more widely known. Second, because they express essential and fundamental beliefs that are held not by any one Catholic alone, but by the Catholic Church as a whole, transmitted through the Magisterium of the pope and the bishops. This Magisterium was established by Christ himself, to confirm the faith of individual believers in him so that down through the centuries and in various parts of the world all may profess one and the same Catholic faith.

Why are the topics presented in dialogue form?

From an editorial point of view, the topics are presented in the form of a dialogue, with questions followed by briefly summarized answers.

This dialogue form tends to be more inviting for the reader, and also continues a constant and long-standing catechetical tradition in the history of the Church. Many catechisms that have formed entire generations have used, and very fruitfully, this didactical system of question and answer.

It must also not be forgotten that the Christian faith itself, a special gift from God, is a continual dialogue of God with man, and of man with God.

I also think that it corresponds to the needs of the contemporary world, in which journalistic-style interviews are preferred, as well as summarized formulations, partly because of the little time that many people, even those who identify themselves as Catholic, now set aside for the catechetical study of their own faith. And this lack of time unfortunately leads to religious ignorance, which in turn leads to widespread relativism, to an arbitrary subjectivism, and last but not least to a distressing vacuum of knowledge about the contents of the faith, which characterizes not only children and young people in their catechetical journey but also adults in their varied and demanding activities.

What is the purpose of this book?

It may help people to understand better the beauty and the importance of the response that the Christian faith offers to all on some topics that characterize our society even today.

This book contains only some of the elements that make up the rich and mysterious panorama of the Catholic faith, and only some of the problems that are eating away at the world today. At the same time, I want to emphasize that in dealing with the individual topics, I do not intend to present all of their aspects and elements, and therefore I do not mean to give each argument exhaustive and complete treatment, but to offer only a few thoughts, fragments of reflection.

So it is intended both for Christians, whom it may provide with an opportunity for a better and deeper understanding of the elements of their faith, and for anyone who might wish to know what the Catholic Church, through some of its official documents, believes and lives, with the help of God.

His Excellency Raffaello Martinelli
Bishop of Frascati
Frascati, September 12, 2010
First anniversary of my episcopal ordination

I
Announcing Jesus

It is necessary to proclaim Jesus Christ because they ask us to: God the Father, Jesus Christ, the Holy Spirit, the Gospel, the human person, the Christian, the Church, today's society.

✠ **God the Father** asks that the proclamation of his Son Jesus Christ be made to all.

For what reason?

Because God "wills everyone to be saved and to come to knowledge of the truth" (1 Tm 2:4).

Therefore

- He sends his Son Jesus Christ, who is his definitive and perfect Word, and our Savior
- He gives the Holy Spirit, thanks to whom we believe in Christ and invoke God as Father

In what way does God want to make his Son known to all?

God has inscribed in the human heart the desire to know him and to love him, and he does not cease to draw every person to him, through his Son in the Holy Spirit.

At the same time, he entrusts to human beings—whom he has called to belong to his People, the Church—the mission of making his Son known and of communicating the salvation achieved by him.

- **Jesus Christ** came into this world so that all "might have life and have it more abundantly" (Jn 10:10).

How does Christ achieve this mission?

- He proclaims the "Good News" to all, and offers his life, dying on the Cross, "for you and for all, for the remission of sins" (see Mt 26:28).
- Before returning to the Father, he gave this order to his disciples: "Go, therefore, and make disciples of all nations, baptizing them in the name of the Father, and of the Son, and of the holy Spirit" (Mt 28:19).
- He presents himself as different from the others, as unique!

Why is Jesus Christ unique?

Because he is the only Son of God, consubstantial with God his Father: "The Father and I are one" (Jn 10:30). In him, God the Father has told us everything and given us everything.

Therefore he, and only he

- Brings us to know God the Father in a full, perfect, and definitive manner: "Whoever has seen me has seen the Father" (Jn 14:9).
- Gives us, by his Death and Resurrection, true and complete salvation: "There is no salvation through anyone else, nor is there any other name under heaven given to the human race by which we are to be saved" (Acts 4:12). There is "one mediator between God and the human race, Christ Jesus, himself human, who gave himself as ransom for all" (1 Tm 2:5-6).

Does Jesus Christ deprive human beings of anything?

Jesus Christ does not deprive human beings of anything. On the contrary, he

- Gives the new divine life of children of God
- Brings to fulfillment, after purifying it, whatever is true, good, or beautiful in every person and in every religion
- Fully realizes the authentic aspirations of the human person
- "Fully reveals man to man himself and makes his supreme calling clear" (*Gaudium et Spes*, no. 22)
- Opens up new horizons for human beings, showing them the way and giving them the grace to reach them

- Does not diminish, but exalts human freedom and urges it toward its fulfillment, in the joyful encounter with God and in gratuitous and considerate love for the good of all people

✠ *The Holy Spirit* poured out within us by God the Father by means of Jesus Christ dead and risen impels us to be messengers, so that all "should know you, the only true God, and the one whom you sent, Jesus Christ" (Jn 17:3).

With his light and his grace, humanity can, in Christ, "find, in unsuspected fullness, everything that it is gropingly searching for concerning God, man and his destiny, life and death, and truth," as John Paul II recalls in the encyclical *Redemptoris Missio* (no. 8).

✠ *The Gospel* must be proclaimed to all. Why?

- Because it is capable of
  - Exciting people of any age, culture, and language
  - Permeating every form of life that does not exclude it by its very nature. And this is because the Word of Christ is not bound "exclusively and indissolubly to any race or nation, nor to any particular way of life or any customary pattern of living, ancient or recent" (*Gaudium et Spes*, no. 58). The Gospel is for all cultures, and all of these can be "fermented" by the Gospel: like the seed that falls on ground where it is able to germinate and bear fruit; or like the leaven that leavens the whole dough, or the salt that gives flavor to the food, or the dew and the rain that permit every kind of plant to grow.

- "The good news of Christ constantly renews the life and culture of fallen man. It combats and removes the errors and evils resulting from sinful allurements which are a perpetual threat. It never ceases to purify and elevate the morality of peoples. By riches coming from above, it makes fruitful, as it were from within, the spiritual qualities and gifts of every people and of every age" (*Gaudium et Spes*, no. 58). The Christian message is not only an *informative* message, but a *performative* one. This means that the Christian faith can never be sealed off in the abstract world of theory but must be brought down into a concrete historical experience that reaches human beings in the deepest truth of their existence (see *Spe Salvi*, no. 2).

✠ *Human persons*, precisely because they are capable of dialoguing with their Creator, have the right and the duty to

- Hear the Truth in the most authentic, complete manner possible: the "Good News" of God who reveals and gives himself in Christ. In this way, people fully realize their vocation.
- Proclaim the Truth, to share one's faith with others. It is characteristic of human beings that they want and in practice try to help others to share in the gifts that they have received and that they appreciate.
- Live their lives to the full: "One does not live by bread alone, but by every word that comes forth from the mouth of God" (Mt 4:4).

Why do people need the proclamation of Christ?

Because Christ

- Liberates people from sin and makes them children of God
- Reveals to people their own complete and original identity
- Offers salvation to every person and to the whole person
- Proclaims indispensable values that are for the sake of the good of all
- Purifies and liberates, elevates and matures, perfects and completes (*purificat, roborat, et elevat: Lumen Gentium*, no. 13)
- Has an extraordinary power of attraction and persuasion, even over people today. This is why it is necessary to proclaim to all, in a serene and positive way, Christian Truth in its integrity, in its completeness, in its harmony, and—why not?—in its beauty as well, so captivating to people today. This will make it possible for people to know and accept that *splendor veritatis*, which is Christ himself.

✠ *The Christian*, every Christian as such, has the right and the duty to proclaim Jesus Christ.

What is the foundation of this right/duty?

This right/duty

- Is based on religious freedom, the natural right of every person, a fundamental element of all freedoms and the ultimate criterion of their preservation
- Is a profound demand of the life of God within the person. The need to proclaim the Gospel to all arises within the Christian from the urge to share with others the original, specific, unique gift of faith that one has received from God. Faith is intensely and essentially personal, but it is never private, it cannot be confined within the walls of the home.
- Is based on the command of Christ: "Whoever believes and is baptized will be saved; whoever does not believe will be condemned" (Mk 16:15-16).
- Is indispensable in order that others may know and accept Christ to obtain salvation. In fact, in order to believe in him one must hear of him, which requires someone who, after coming to know him, proclaims him to others. In fact: "How can they call on him in whom they have not believed? And how can they believe in him of whom they have not heard? And how can they hear without someone to preach?" (Rom 10:14).

✠ *The Catholic Church*, always and everywhere, has proclaimed Christ.

Why, and in what way?

- The Church exists not to proclaim itself, or a new or different religion, but to proclaim and communicate

Christ. The Church cannot and does not want to change anything of what Christ proclaimed and is contained in Sacred Scripture and Tradition.

■ The first and main duty of the entire Church in its two millennia of tradition has been and is the *Traditio Evangelii* (the communication of the Gospel, evangelization). And "there is no true evangelization if the name, the teaching, the life, the promises, the Kingdom and the mystery of Jesus of Nazareth, the Son of God are not proclaimed" (*Evangelii Nuntiandi*, no. 22).

■ It is the right and duty of the Church, of the whole Church, to proclaim the whole Gospel to the whole person and to every person, in the most faithful way possible, avoiding reductionism and ambiguities, and making this proclamation the first priority in its concerns and activities.

■ The Church cannot and does not want to change anything of what Christ proclaimed and is contained in Sacred Scripture and Sacred Tradition. Its task is to proclaim and interpret this *depositum fidei*, to develop it, explore it, and present it more extensively: "For the deposit of faith itself, or the truths which are contained in our venerable doctrine, are one thing; another thing is the way in which they are expressed, with however the same meaning and signification" (Blessed John XXIII, Address of October 11, 1962). "What Christ willed, we also will. What was, still is. What the Church has taught down through the centuries, we also teach. In simple terms that which was assumed, is now explicit; that which was uncertain, is now clarified; that which was meditated upon, discussed and sometimes argued over, is now put together in one clear formulation" (Pope Paul VI, Address of November 21, 1964).

- The Apostles themselves, at the beginning of the life of the Church, made their first priority the proclamation of Christ: "It is not right for us to neglect the word of God to serve at table. Brothers, select from among you seven reputable men, filled with the Spirit and wisdom, whom we shall appoint to this task, whereas we shall devote ourselves to prayer and to the ministry of the word" (Acts 6:2-4).

- After the Apostles, many others have made these words of St. Paul their own: "If I preach the gospel, this is no reason for me to boast, for an obligation has been imposed on me, and woe to me if I do not preach it!" (1 Cor 9:16). It is a duty and an honor to preach the Gospel!

- Every activity of the Church (even if it is humanitarian, in defense of human rights, of peace, etc.) must be inseparable from the commitment to help everyone to encounter Christ in the faith. This norm of conduct has been valid throughout the entire history of the Church and will continue to be so forever. Throughout history, there have been countless initiatives to spread the Gospel, and these profoundly characterize the entire life of the People of God: they lead to the encounter with Christ.

- The evangelizing action of the Church can never be lacking, because the presence of the Lord with the power of the Holy Spirit will never be lacking, according to his promise: "I am with you always, until the end of the age" (Mt 28:20).

- The Church, in proclaiming Christ as the Truth and Salvation of humanity, is meeting the need of those who sincerely seek this Truth and Salvation, establishing with them a purposeful dialogue centered on the love of the truth. Evangelizing is an exquisite act of charity toward the person.

- Everyone is called to holiness in the Church. Holiness means following in the footsteps of Christ, who came to proclaim salvation to all and has entrusted this mission of proclamation to every Christian and to the Church.

- The Church also proclaims Christ through the courageous witness of its faithful who accept even martyrdom in order not to renounce their faith. The Carthusian monk Lanspergius (1489-1539) wrote, "The precious death of its martyrs and its saints has led to the birth of a great multitude of Christians. In fact, the Christian religion has never been annihilated by the persecution of tyrants, nor by the unjustifiable murder of innocents; instead, it has been greatly increased every time."

✠ *Today's society* needs the proclamation of the Gospel.

How is this need manifested?

- The contemporary cultural context, marked by both widespread relativism and the temptation to simplistic pragmatism, demands more than ever the courageous proclamation of the Truth that saves the human person and society. It must not be forgotten that behind many of the phenomena of our time, apparently far from the faith and from Christ, there is a question, an anticipation, a desire to which the only true, definitive, exhaustive response is Christ.

- The ethical social order needs to be illuminated by the proclamation of Christ. And this is because, as Pope John XXIII rightly affirmed in the encyclical *Mater et Magistra*, the human person "demands, therefore, a moral and religious order; and it is this order—and not considerations of a purely extraneous, material order—which has the greatest validity in the solution of problems relating to his life as an individual and as a member of society, and problems concerning individual states and their inter-relations" (no. 208).

- The proclamation of the Gospel helps us to understand the historical-cultural heritage of many peoples and nations. In fact, the principles of the Gospel are an integral part of this heritage: the history, culture, and civilization of many generations, down through the centuries, have been impregnated with Christianity and intimately connected with the journey of the Church. This is witnessed to not only by the countless works of art that have adorned different places all over the world, but also by the traditions, the customs, and the habits that characterize the thought and action of the different peoples.

■ Although today's world facilitates communication, it doubts the capacity of the person to know the truth, or even denies the possibility of the existence of one sole Truth, and yet at the same time manifests in various ways a need for the absolute, an unquenchable thirst for Truth and for certitude. The proclamation of the Gospel meets these needs and is capable of bringing them full satisfaction. As Blessed Teresa of Calcutta affirmed: "The first poverty of people is that of not knowing Christ. People are hungry for God. People are thirsty for love."

■ The proclamation of the Gospel, John Paul II affirms in the encyclical *Slavorum Apostoli*, "does not lead to the impoverishment or extinction of those things which every individual, people and nation and every culture throughout history recognizes and brings into being as goodness, truth and beauty. On the contrary, it strives to assimilate and to develop all these values: to live them with magnanimity and joy and to perfect them by the mysterious and ennobling light of Revelation" (no. 18). For these and other reasons, it is absolutely necessary to proclaim Jesus Christ who died and rose for the salvation of all.

✠

For more on this topic, see the following pontifical documents:

Pope John Paul II, *Redemptoris Missio; Slavorum Apostoli*
Catechism of the Catholic Church, nos. 422-682
Compendium of the CCC, nos. 79-135
Congregation for the Doctrine of the Faith, *Dominus Iesus*
Vatican Council II, *Gaudium et Spes*
Pope Paul VI, *Lumen Gentium*

II
Evangelization

What does it mean to evangelize?

✠ It means proclaiming the Lord Jesus in word and action, becoming an instrument of his presence and action in the world.

The primary objective of evangelization is therefore that of helping everyone to encounter Christ in the faith. "Social issues and the Gospel are inseparable. When we bring people only knowledge, ability, technical competence and tools, we bring them too little" (Pope Benedict XVI, Homily at Neue Messe, Munich, September 10, 2006).

✠ This encounter with Christ involves the whole person (intelligence, will, emotions, activities, plans) and every person: the object of evangelization is the whole of humanity.

Why evangelize?

For various and complementary reasons:

✠ In obedience to the command of Christ, who said: "Go into the whole world and proclaim the gospel to every creature.

Whoever believes and is baptized will be saved; whoever does not believe will be condemned" (Mk 16:15-16). "As the Father has sent me, so I send you" (Jn 20:21; see 17:18). This command of Christ finds its foundation and its justification in his infinite love for the eternal salvation of humanity.

✠   To follow the example of the Apostles, who, "prompted by the Spirit, invited all to change their lives, to be converted and to be baptized" (*Redemptoris Missio*, no. 47)

✠   To actualize a threefold love: of the Word of God, of the Church, and of the world

✠   To satisfy the right of every person: "Every person has the right to hear the 'Good News' of the God who reveals and gives himself in Christ, so that each one can live out in its fullness his or her proper calling" (*Redemptoris Missio*, no. 46). This is a right conferred by the Lord on every person, by virtue of which every man and every woman can truly say with St. Paul: Jesus Christ "has loved me and given himself up for me" (Gal 2:20). The heart of every person yearns for, waits for the encounter with Christ. To this right corresponds the duty of evangelization: "If I preach the gospel, this is no reason for me to boast, for an obligation has been imposed on me, and woe to me if I do not preach it!" (1 Cor 9:16; see Rom 10:14). "*Caritas Christi urget nos*—the love of Christ impels us" (2 Cor 5:14) to proclaim the Gospel to everyone.

✠   To share with others, in respect and dialogue, the gifts we have received: "The acceptance of the Good News in faith is thus dynamically ordered to such a communication. The truth which saves one's life inflames the heart of the one who has received it with a love of neighbor that motivates him to pass on to others in freedom what he has freely been given . . . The Church wants everyone to share in these goods so that they may possess the fullness of truth and the fullness of the means of salvation, in order 'to enter into the freedom of the glory of the children of God' (Rom 8:21) . . . This experience of sharing, a characteristic of true friendship, is a valuable occasion for witnessing and for Christian proclamation" (*Doctrinal Note on Some Aspects of Evangelization* [hereafter *Aspects of Evangelization*], nos. 7-8).

✠ To actualize an original and indispensable form of service to the person: "The proclamation of and witness to the Gospel are the first service that Christians can render to every person and to the entire human race, called as they are to communicate to all God's love, which was fully manifested in Jesus Christ, the one Redeemer of the world" (Pope Benedict XVI, Address on the 40th anniversary of the conciliar decree "Ad Gentes," March 11, 2006).

✠ To help people to escape from the various forms of desert in which they live: "The desert of God's darkness, the emptiness of souls no longer aware of their dignity or the goal of human life . . . the Church as a whole and all her Pastors, like Christ, must set out to lead people out of the desert, towards the place of life, towards friendship with the Son of God, towards the One who gives us life, and life in abundance" (Pope Benedict XVI, Homily during Mass for the inauguration of the pontificate, April 24, 2005).

✠ Evangelizing is not only a duty, but also an indispensable right, an integral expression of the religious freedom of the person, as well as the right of the person to seek complete happiness. As Paul VI used to say, "Christianity is not easy [*facile*], but happy [*felice*]."

✠ In this regard, see also Chapter I, "Announcing Jesus."

What objections are made to evangelization?

1. Is evangelization an attack on the religious freedom of the person?

✠ Here it is necessary to remember above all that the freedom of the person

- Exists in strict relation with the truth
  - Freedom is not indifference, but a reaching for the truth, for goodness (*bonum et verum convertuntur*: the good and the true coincide). Separating freedom from truth is one of the expressions "which, recognizing nothing as definitive, leaves as the ultimate criterion only the self with its desires and under the semblance of freedom, becomes a prison for each one" (Pope Benedict XVI, Address to the participants in the Ecclesial Diocesan Convention of Rome, June 6, 2005).
  - Denying that the possibility to know the truth exists, or that the truth has an "exclusive character and assuming that truth reveals itself equally in different doctrines, even if they contradict

one another" (*Fides et Ratio*, no. 5), deprives the human person of "what in a unique way draws his intelligence and enthralls his heart" (*Aspects of Evangelization*, no. 4).

■ Needs, in the search for truth, the help of others

● "From birth, therefore, [human beings] are immersed in traditions which give them not only a language and a cultural formation but also a range of truths in which they believe almost instinctively . . . There are in the life of a human being many more truths which are simply believed than truths which are acquired by way of personal verification" (*Fides et Ratio*, no. 31).

● Truth is attained in part by entrusting oneself to those who can guarantee the certainty and authenticity of the truth itself: "There is no doubt that the capacity to entrust oneself and one's life to another person and the decision to do so are among the most significant and expressive human acts" (*Fides et Ratio*, no 33).

✠ After affirming the duty and the right of every person to seek the truth in religious matters, Vatican Council II adds: "Truth, however, is to be sought after in a manner proper to the dignity of the human person and his social nature. The inquiry is to be free, carried on with the aid of teaching or instruction, communication, and dialogue. In the course of these, men explain to one another the truth they have discovered, or think they have discovered, in order thus to assist one another in the quest for truth." In any case, the truth "cannot impose itself except by virtue of its own truth" (*Dignitatis Humanae*, nos. 3, 1).

✠ "Therefore, to lead a person's intelligence and freedom in honesty to the encounter with Christ and his Gospel is not an inappropriate encroachment, but rather a legitimate endeavor and a service capable of making human relationships more fruitful . . . Fully belonging to Christ, who is the Truth, and entering the Church do not lessen human freedom, but rather exalt it and direct it towards its fulfillment, in a love that is freely given and which overflows with care for the good of all people" (*Aspects of Evangelization*, nos. 5-7).

2. Since the non-Christian can be saved, is evangelization useless?

"Although non-Christians can be saved through the grace which God bestows in 'ways known to him,' the Church cannot fail to recognize that such persons are lacking a tremendous benefit in this world: to know the true face of God and the friendship of Jesus Christ, God-with-us. Indeed 'there is nothing more beautiful than to be surprised by the Gospel, by the encounter with Christ. There is nothing more beautiful than to know him and to speak to others of our friendship with him.' The revelation of the fundamental truths about God, about the human person and the world, is a great good for every human person, while living in darkness without the truths about ultimate questions is an evil and is often at the root of suffering and slavery which can at times be grievous. This is why St. Paul does not hesitate to describe conversion to the Christian faith as liberation 'from the power of darkness' and entrance into 'the kingdom of his beloved Son in whom we have redemption and the forgiveness of our sins' (Col 1:13-14)" (*Aspects of Evangelization*, no. 7).

3. Does evangelization express intolerance? Is it perhaps a threat to peace?

"Those who make such claims are overlooking the fact that the fullness of the gift of truth, which God makes by revealing himself to man, respects the freedom which he himself created as an indelible mark of human nature: a freedom which is not indifference, but which is rather directed towards truth. This kind of respect is a requirement of the Catholic faith itself and of the love of Christ; it is a constitutive element of evangelization and, therefore, a good which is to be promoted inseparably with the commitment to making the fullness of salvation, which God offers to the human race in the Church, known and freely embraced" (*Aspects of Evangelization*, no. 10).

How does evangelization take place?

Evangelization takes place

✠ In respect for the freedom of the person: "The Church strictly forbids forcing anyone to embrace the faith, or alluring or enticing people by unworthy techniques. By the same token, she also strongly insists on a person's right not to be deterred from the faith by unjust vexations on the part of others" (*Ad Gentes*, no. 13). "From the very origins of the Church the disciples of Christ strove to convert men to faith in Christ as the Lord—not, however, by the use of coercion or by devices unworthy of the gospel, but by the power, above all, of the Word of God" (*Dignitatis Humanae*, no. 11).

✠   Through private and public preaching of the Gospel, and also through the creation of works of public significance

✠   Through words and through the testimony of life, which go together. "All Christians are called to this witness, and in this way they can be real evangelizers. We are thinking especially of the responsibility incumbent on immigrants in the country that receives them. Nevertheless this always remains insufficient, because even the finest witness will prove ineffective in the long run if it is not explained, justified—what Peter called always having 'your answer ready for people who ask you the reason for the hope that you all have' (1 Pt 3:15)—and made explicit by a clear and unequivocal proclamation of the Lord Jesus" (*Evangelii Nuntiandi*, nos. 21-22).

✠   With trust in the power of the Holy Spirit and of the truth itself when proclaimed

✠   In the gift of self to the point of martyrdom: "It is precisely martyrdom that gives credibility to witnesses, who seek neither power nor advantage, but instead lay down their lives for Christ. Before all the world, they display an unarmed strength brimming with love for all people, which is bestowed on those who follow Christ unto the total gift of their existence. So it is that Christians, from the very dawn of Christianity up until our own time have suffered persecution on account of the Gospel, as Jesus himself foretold: 'If they persecuted me, they will also persecute you' (Jn 15:20)" (*Aspects of Evangelization*, no. 8).

Who is responsible for evangelizing?

Every Christian. "The words of Jesus 'go therefore and teach all nations, baptizing them in the name of the Father, the Son and the Holy Spirit, teaching them to observe all that I have commanded you' (Mt 28:19-20), are directed to everyone in the Church, each according to his own vocation. At the present time, with so many people in the world living in different types of desert, above all, in the 'desert of God's darkness, the emptiness of souls no longer aware of their dignity or the goal of human life,' Pope Benedict XVI has recalled to the world that 'the Church as a whole and all her Pastors, like Christ, must set out to lead people out of the desert, towards the place of life, towards friendship with the Son of God, towards the One who gives us life, and life in abundance.' This apostolic commitment is an inalienable right and duty, an expression of religious liberty, with its corresponding ethical-social and ethical-political dimensions. It is a right which in some parts of the world, unfortunately, has not yet been recognized and which in others is not respected in practice. He who announces the Gospel participates in the charity of Christ, who loved us and gave himself up for us (cf. Eph 5:2); he is his ambassador and he pleads in the name of Christ: let yourselves to be reconciled with God! (cf. 2 Cor 5:20). It is a charity which is an expression of the gratitude that flows from the heart when it opens to the love given in Jesus Christ" (*Aspects of Evangelization*, nos. 10-11).

In what way does evangelization enrich the Church itself?

✠ In proclaiming Jesus Christ to every person within his or her sociocultural context, the Church

- Takes on, in Christ, the countless gifts of the people of all times and places in human history (see *Slavorum Apostoli*, no. 18)
- "Is enriched with forms of expression and values in the various sectors of Christian life" (*Redemptoris Missio*, no. 52)
- "Comes to know and to express better the mystery of Christ, all the while being motivated to continual renewal" (*Redemptoris Missio*, no. 52)
- Discovers and expresses better the potentialities of the Gospel that were little known and explained before, and in this way the "tradition which comes from the apostles develops in the Church with the help of the Holy Spirit" (*Dei Verbum*, no. 8)

✠ "In this way, the Pentecost-event continues in history, in the unity of one and the same faith, enriched by the diversity of languages and cultures" (*Aspects of Evangelization*, no. 6).

✠ "The incorporation of new members into the Church is not the expansion of a power-group, but rather entrance into the network of friendship with Christ which connects heaven and earth, different continents and ages" (*Aspects of Evangelization*, no. 9).

Should evangelization also be directed to non-Catholic Christians?

✠ This kind of evangelization (which is called "ecumenism"), on the part of every Catholic Christian, involves

- True respect for our separated brothers and sisters, especially for their freedom, tradition, and spiritual riches
- Prayer, penance, and study
- A full witness to and proclamation of one's own faith
- A sincere spirit of cooperation in all areas—practical, social, religious, and cultural
- "A respectful dialogue of charity and truth, a dialogue which is not only an exchange of ideas, but also of gifts, in order that the fullness of the means of salvation can be offered to one's partners in dialogue" (*Aspects of Evangelization*, no. 12). An ecumenism, therefore, of truth and of charity: the two are intimately connected. (See, in this regard Chapter VIII, "Ecumenism.")

✠ "In this connection, it needs also to be recalled that if a non-Catholic Christian, for reasons of conscience and having been convinced of Catholic truth, asks to enter into the full communion of the Catholic Church, this is to be respected as the work of the Holy Spirit and as an expression of freedom of conscience and of religion. In such a case, it would not be a question of proselytism in the negative sense that has been attributed to this term" (*Aspects of Evangelization*, no. 12).

✠

For more on these topics, see the following pontifical documents:

Vatican Council II, *Dei Verbum*; *Dignitatis Humanae*; *Ad Gentes*; *Gaudium et Spes*; *Unitatis Redintegratio*

Paul VI, *Evangelii Nuntiandi*, December 8, 1975

John Paul II, *Slavorum Apostoli*, June 2, 1985; *Redemptoris Missio*, December 7, 1990; *Ut Unum Sint*, May 25, 1995

Benedict XVI, Homily during Mass for the inauguration of the pontificate, April 24, 2005; *Deus Caritas Est*, December 25, 2005

Congregation for the Doctrine of the Faith, *Dominus Iesus*, August 6, 2000; *Doctrinal Note on Some Aspects of Evangelization*, December 3, 2007

III
The Four Gospels

What does the word "Gospel" mean?

✠ "Gospel" comes from the Greek word "ευαγγέλιον" (*evangelion*), which means "glad tidings" or "good news." These *glad tidings* concern the life and preaching of Jesus Christ, the Only-Begotten Son of God made man.

✠ "In Jesus' time, the term 'gospel' was used by Roman emperors for their proclamations. Independently of their content, they were described as 'good news' or announcements of salvation, because the emperor was considered lord of the world and his every edict as a portent of good. Thus, the application of this phrase to Jesus' preaching had a strongly critical meaning, as if to say God, and not the emperor, is Lord of the world, and the true Gospel is that of Jesus Christ" (Pope Benedict XVI, *Angelus*, January 27, 2008).

How many Gospels are there, and which are they?

There are four: the Gospel of Matthew (Mt), of Mark (Mk), of Luke (Lk), and of John (Jn). They are part of Sacred Scripture, specifically of the New Testament. They therefore belong to the canon of Scripture, which is "the complete list of the sacred writings which the Church has come to recognize through Apostolic Tradition. The Canon consists of 46 books of the Old Testament and 27 of the New" (*Compendium of the Catechism of the Catholic Church* [*Compendium of the CCC*], no. 20). The Church is the solid and stable criterion of the canonicity of Sacred Scripture. The Catholic Church, guided by the Spirit of truth, is the authentic custodian of the deposit of Revelation and the rule of faith. In fact, it "established which books are to be held as authentic in the canon of the Bible" (Duns Scotus, *Ordinatio* I d.5 n. 26, ed. Vat. IV 25).

When were they written?

The four Gospels were written between AD 60 and 100.

Why are there only four of them?

✠ There are only four because the Apostolic Tradition led the Church to discern that these four Gospels, and only these four, should be included in the list of sacred books.

✠ St. Irenaeus, bishop of Lyons and martyr, states in a famous passage written at the end of the second century that "since the world has four regions and there are four principal winds . . . the Word who created all things . . . in revealing himself to human beings, has given us a Gospel that is four-fold, but unified by a single Spirit" (*Against Heresies* III 11, 8).

What is the Apostolic Tradition?

The Apostolic Tradition has two branches: the living transmission of the Word of God (also called simply "Tradition") and Sacred Scripture, which is the same proclamation of salvation set down in writing.

What relationship exists between Tradition and Sacred Scripture?

Tradition and Sacred Scripture are in close contact and communication. Both make the mystery of Christ present and fruitful within the Church, and both arise from the same divine source: they constitute a single sacred deposit of faith from which the Church draws its own certainty about all revealed truths. "Therefore both sacred tradition and sacred Scripture are to be accepted and venerated with the same sense of devotion and reverence" (*Dei Verbum*, no. 9).

What relationship exists among Scripture, Tradition, and Magisterium?

They are so closely united that none of them exists without the others. "Working together, each in its own way, under the action of the one Holy Spirit, they all contribute effectively to the salvation of souls" (*Compendium of the CCC*, no. 17; see also nos. 12-14).

What do we know about the authors of the four Gospels?

According to tradition, this is what we know about the authors of the four Gospels:

- Mark: He is often identified with the "young man . . . wearing nothing but a linen cloth about his body" who tried to follow Jesus after his arrest (Mk 14:51-52). Afterward he became a disciple of St. Peter; he also followed St. Paul on one of his missionary journeys.
- Matthew: Also called Levi, he was one of the Apostles. He was a publican, or tax collector. Jesus called him while he was sitting at the customs post.
- Luke: A disciple of St. Paul, he followed him on some of his voyages. He is also believed to be the author of the Acts of the Apostles. He was a physician, probably from Antioch. According to tradition, he also painted a portrait of the Virgin Mary.
- John: In his Gospel, he often refers to himself as "the disciple whom Jesus loved." "Although tradition identified this person as John, the son of Zebedee, most modern scholars find that the evidence does not support this" (NAB, Gospel according to John, Introduction).

What importance do the Gospels have for Christians?

"Within the New Testament the four Gospels of Matthew, Mark, Luke and John are the heart of all the Scriptures because they are the principle witness to the life and teaching of Jesus. As such, they hold a unique place in the Church" (*Compendium of the CCC*, no. 22).

✠ At the same time, it must be remembered that

- The Word of God is not limited to Sacred Scripture, which is indeed its privileged witness, but this Word transcends even its biblical incarnation. In fact, the Word of God is a Person—Jesus Christ—who is thus the perfect and definitive incarnation of the Word of God.

- Christianity cannot be defined as a "religion of the Book" per se, even though the biblical testimony about Jesus is important, and in fact indispensable. Christianity is more precisely the "religion of the person": the person of Jesus Christ, through whom God the Father is revealed and communicated in the Holy Spirit.

How did the Gospels take shape?

✠ Three stages can be distinguished in the formation of the Gospels:

1. *The life and teaching of Jesus.* Jesus did not leave anything in writing. He preached and taught, he chose and formed disciples, particularly the Twelve Apostles. They spent three years listening to him. It must be emphasized in this regard that preaching and teaching from memory was a normal practice at the time and arose from the fact that writing was impractical under ordinary conditions.

2. *Oral tradition.* "Indeed, after the ascension of the Lord the apostles handed on to their hearers what He had said and done. This they did with that clearer understanding which they enjoyed after they had been instructed by the events of Christ's risen life and taught by the light of the Spirit of truth" (*Dei Verbum*, no. 19). So the Apostles fulfilled what Jesus had ordered them to do: "Go, therefore, and make disciples of all nations, baptizing them in the name of the Father, and of the Son, and of the holy Spirit" (Mt 28:19). In carrying out this commandment of Christ, they proclaimed aloud the episodes that they had witnessed during their life with Jesus, repeating, especially to those who had not known him, his words and teachings. In this way, the memories and stories about Jesus, as well as his words and miracles, handed down in a constant and faithful manner, took on a very precise literary form. For example, very soon after the Death and Resurrection of Jesus, around the year AD 40, the Church was singing the famous hymn contained in the Letter of St. Paul to the Philippians: "[Jesus Christ], though he was in the form of God, did not regard equality with God something to be grasped" (Phil 2:6).

    About this preaching, it must be noted:

    ■   The Christian community *did not create the content* of the preaching, but elaborated its literary form.

- This content is based on the authoritative testimony of eyewitnesses.
- It was strictly controlled by the apostolic community in Jerusalem, which was concerned about being faithful to the memory of Jesus.

3. *The written Gospels*. The apostolic teachings about Jesus did not remain pure oral teaching, but starting very early, gradually, they were put down in writing. This took place between AD 60 and 100. "The sacred authors wrote the four Gospels, selecting some things from the many which had been handed on by word of mouth or in writing, reducing some of them to a synthesis, explicating some things in view of the situation of their churches, and preserving the form of proclamation but always in such fashion that they told us the honest truth about Jesus" (*Dei Verbum*, no. 19). The reason for this setting down in writing of what they had been proclaiming orally is to be found in some of the *needs* of the first Christian communities:

- The celebration of the *liturgy*. In order to celebrate, they needed texts that could be read.
- *Catechesis*, the formation of believers. Catechists needed reference texts on which to base their own teaching.
- The missionary activity of proclaiming the Gospel to nonbelievers, which at the very least required having access to *reminders* of the teachings and significant sayings of Jesus

- Determining the *practical moral behavior* of Christians in the encounter with different cultures and lifestyles
- *Defense against the accusations, slander, and misunderstandings* to which the communities were subjected, on the part of both Jews and pagans

✠ There is continuity between the preaching of Jesus, the apostolic preaching, and the presentation of these in the Gospels.

✠ In the narration of the Gospels, there is a very close connection with the events as they actually happened: "It is of the very essence of biblical faith to be about real historical events. It [the Bible] does not tell stories symbolizing suprahistorical truths, but is based on history, history that took place here on this earth . . . We are not meant to regard Jesus' activity as taking place in some sort of mythical 'anytime,' which can mean always or never. It is a precisely datable historical event having the full weight that real historical happenings have" (*Jesus of Nazareth*, New York: Doubleday [2007], xi, 11).

✠ All of this took place under the guidance of the Holy Spirit, as Jesus himself had promised during his earthly life: "I have told you this while I am with you. The Advocate, the holy Spirit that the Father will send in my name—he will teach you everything and remind you of all that [I] told you" (Jn 14:25-26). "He will glorify me, because he will take from what is mine and declare it to you" (Jn 16:14).

How were the Gospels handed down over the centuries?

✠   There is above all the manuscript transmission (starting in AD 60) in Koine Greek (a simplified form of Greek that was commonly used at the time). The most ancient manuscripts of the Gospels, like all of the New Testament, have come down to us in Greek. The Bodmer papyrus XIV-XV (P 75), dated to between 175 and 225, is the most ancient manuscript of the Gospels of Luke and John known to have survived. After this, between the second and third century, the Gospels were translated from Greek into Latin (*vetus latina*): the Codex Vaticanus ("Vaticano greco 1209"), from the fourth century, is the most ancient complete text of the Bible to have come down to us. Following the invention of movable type (beginning in 1516) manuscript transmission was replaced with print.

✠   Already in the second half of the second century, St. Justin, in his *Apology* written in 160, affirms that the memories of the apostles were called Gospels. It is the first evidence of the transition from the Gospel as preaching and proclamation to the Gospel as written text.

Are the Gospels of apostolic origin?

The Church affirms as an article of faith that the Gospels come from the apostles. "The Church has always and everywhere held and continues to hold that the four Gospels are of apostolic origin. For what the apostles preached in fulfillment of the commission of Christ, afterwards they themselves and apostolic men, under the inspiration of the divine Spirit, handed on to us in writing: the foundation of faith, namely, the fourfold Gospel, according to Matthew, Mark, Luke, and John" (*Dei Verbum*, no. 18).

In what sense are the Gospels historical?

✠ The Gospels are historical in that they faithfully report the works and words of Jesus, in the light of his Death and Resurrection, under the influence of the Holy Spirit. "Holy Mother Church has firmly and with absolute constancy held, and continues to hold, that the four Gospels just named, whose historical character the Church unhesitatingly asserts, faithfully hand on what Jesus Christ, while living among men, really did and taught for their eternal salvation until the day He was taken up into heaven" (*Dei Verbum*, no. 19).

✠ It must be kept in mind that the Gospels were written in a historical period (the first century AD) in which the apostles and many other people who had known, listened to, and lived with Jesus were still alive, as were people who had known and lived with the apostles. They were therefore able to verify whether what was being preached and written corresponded to the truth or not. And it must not be forgotten in this regard that many of these people accepted martyrdom rather than renouncing their fidelity to Christ (see for example the persecution undergone by many Christians in the year 64 because of Nero).

✠ In order to guarantee the historicity of the facts as such, there are also various complementary criteria (like the criteria of multiple attestation, non-contradiction, continuity and discontinuity, consistency, etc.) that are able to provide moral certainty of historicity for most of the events narrated in the Gospels.

What are the criteria of the authenticity of the Gospels?

✠   The fundamental criterion: the recognition of the Church as divinely assisted by the Holy Spirit. This recognition was given by the first ecclesial community in the first century AD and has always been reconfirmed by the Church over the following centuries, up until today.

✠   Objective criteria:

- Their apostolic origin
- Absolute fidelity to what Jesus said and did
- The testimony of those who were eyewitnesses

In what sense are the Gospels inspired books?

"Those divinely revealed realities which are contained and presented in sacred Scripture have been committed to writing under the inspiration of the Holy Spirit. Holy Mother Church, relying on the belief of the apostles, holds that the books of both the Old and New Testament in their entirety, with all their parts, are sacred and canonical because, having been written under the inspiration of the Holy Spirit (see Jn 20:31; 2 Tm 3:16; 2 Pt 1:19-20, 3:15-16) they have God as their author and have been handed on as such to the Church herself. In composing the sacred books, God chose men and while employed by Him they made use of their powers and abilities, so that with Him acting in them and through them, they, as true authors, consigned to writing everything and only those things which He wanted" (*Dei Verbum*, no. 11).

How do we know that the Gospels teach the truth?

Because God himself is their author. Therefore they teach without error those truths that are necessary for our salvation. "Therefore, since everything asserted by the inspired authors or sacred writers must be held to be asserted by the Holy Spirit, it follows that the books of Scripture must be acknowledged as teaching firmly, faithfully, and without error that truth which God wanted put into the sacred writings for the sake of our salvation. Therefore 'all Scripture is inspired by God and useful for teaching, for reproving, for correcting, for instruction in justice; that the man of God may be perfect, equipped for every good work' (2 Tm 3:16-17, Greek text)" (*Dei Verbum*, no. 11).

What are some of the characteristics of the individual Gospels?

✠ *The Gospel according to Mark*: This is believed to be the oldest of the four Gospels. It dates back to the year AD 64, or thirty-four years after the probable date of the Death of Jesus.

It has more of a narrative tone: rich in details, it paints a good picture of the Holy Land at the time of Jesus. The intended audience of the work was the non-Jewish Christian, probably of Rome. The author is the Mark known to Peter, who later accompanied Paul and Barnabas. The Gospel of

Mark is characterized in part by the use of the term "way": the journey of Jesus to Jerusalem, toward the fulfillment of the Paschal Mystery.

✠   *The Gospel according to Matthew*: This was intended for an audience of Jewish origin, as can be seen by the frequency with which the Old Testament is cited. According to Christian tradition, the author was one of the Twelve Apostles, who is called Matthew (the tax collector) in some passages, and Levi in others. This Gospel, rich in parables and with five long sermons of Jesus, including the famous Sermon on the Mount (5:1-7, 29), is generally considered to have the greatest focus on moral values, and for centuries has inspired people of every culture and religion.

✠   *The Gospel according to Luke*: This is one part of a larger work, the other part being the Acts of the Apostles. Written by the same author, they use the same style and are addressed to the same recipient, a certain Theophilus, who is not mentioned anywhere else (the name Theophilus means "friend of God" in Greek). According to tradition, its author is Luke, who accompanied St. Paul on some of his voyages. The heart of the work is the activity of Jesus in Jerusalem, the preaching of the beginning of a new era, the redemption of humanity, and love for the poor.

✠   *The Gospel according to John*: This is very different from the others, even in terms of style. There are far fewer parables, fewer miracles, and no mention of the institution of the Eucharist, of the Our Father, or of the Beatitudes. There are new expressions referring to Jesus (e.g., "Word of God").

A great Christian writer of the third century, Origen, said of the fourth Gospel, "the flower of all Sacred Scripture is the Gospel, and the flower of the Gospel is the one transmitted to us by John, the profound and inmost meaning of which no one will ever fully grasp."

What characteristics do the Gospels present on the whole?

✠ About the *sources*, it is necessary to emphasize

- The careful verification of historical events. This is what Luke says in this regard in his Gospel: "Since many have undertaken to compile a narrative of the events that have been fulfilled among us, just as those who were eyewitnesses from the beginning and ministers of the word have handed them down to us, I too have decided, after investigating everything accurately anew, to write it down in an orderly sequence for you, most excellent Theophilus, so that you may realize the certainty of the teachings you have received" (1:1-4).

- The eyewitness testimony and the surprising, new experience of some of the people who lived with Jesus

✠ About the *content*:

- The Gospels complete each other, each one emphasizing some particular aspects of the teaching and work of Christ. The differentiation between one Gospel and the other does not undermine the substantial historicity of the person of Jesus, of what he said and did.

- Not only do they contain the Word of God, but they themselves are the Word of God: the Word of God in human words. "For the words of God, expressed in human language, have been made like human discourse, just as of old the Word of the eternal Father, when he took to Himself the weak flesh of humanity, became like other men" (*Dei Verbum*, no. 13). As human works, the Gospels must be studied according to scholarly criteria (of literary and historical criticism), but as the Word of God, they must be read also and above all according to the criteria of faith.

- Jesus Christ is the central content, the primordial and permanent reality, the stable center that unifies and gives solidity to the Gospels, which are the faithful echo of what Jesus said and did. The Gospels form just one book, and this one book is Christ. He is the one who definitively reveals the Father through his very being, through his words and works, through his miracles, through his Death and Resurrection, through the gift of the Holy Spirit.

- The Christian faith is not "a religion of the Book," but of the Word of God, which is not "a written and mute word, but the incarnate and living Word" (St. Bernard of Clairvaux).

- There is a common feature in the presentation of the main events of the life of Jesus: Jesus is presented in his main outlines, in the constants of his teaching and behavior, in the fundamental moments of his public life, in his absolute novelty and originality: "And the Word became flesh and made his dwelling among us, and we saw his glory, the glory as of the Father's only Son, full of grace and truth" (Jn 1:14).

✠ About the *interpretation* of the events: this is done in the light of the Resurrection of Jesus, and put at the service of the lives of believers and of the Church. The Gospels were written in the certitude that the Jesus who died on the Cross is risen, and therefore is always alive and present in the Church. So now, knowledge of the Risen One must come from the past life and teaching of Jesus, not simply as past, but as illuminating with this past the Christ who still lives.

✠ About *finality*:

- The Gospels do not intend to present us with a biography of Jesus. The sacred authors, like the tradition before them, have no interest in a detailed description of the events of the life of Jesus. The details present in the text do not serve as a journalistic description of the events.
- The Gospels do not provide answers for problems of history or science. The truth that Jesus communicates is for our salvation. The Gospels report actions and statements of Jesus that are held to be of significance for salvation.
- The Gospels intend, instead, to express and elicit faith in the Lord Jesus. Being transmitted by believers to elicit and foster faith, the evangelical tradition calls

attention to the significance of these events for the faith. Therefore the truth of an account does not lie in the exact reporting of an event but in grasping the meaning, the value, the lesson contained in the event.

What is the unity that exists between the Old and the New Testaments?

"Scripture is one insofar as the Word of God is one. God's plan of salvation is one, and the divine inspiration of both Testaments is one. The Old Testament prepares for the New and the New Testament fulfills the Old; the two shed light on each other" (*Compendium of the CCC*, no. 23).

What role does Sacred Scripture play in the life of the Church?

"Sacred Scripture gives support and vigor to the life of the Church. For the children of the Church, it is a confirmation of the faith, food for the soul and the fount of the spiritual life. Sacred Scripture is the soul of theology and of pastoral preaching. The Psalmist says that it is 'a lamp to my feet and a light to my path' (Ps 119:105). The Church, therefore, exhorts all to read Sacred Scripture frequently because 'ignorance of the Scriptures is ignorance of Christ' (St. Jerome)" (*Compendium of the CCC*, no. 24).

"The Church has always venerated the divine Scriptures just as she venerates the body of the Lord, since from the table of both the word of God and of the body of Christ she unceasingly receives and offers to the faithful the bread of life, especially in the sacred liturgy. She has always regarded the Scriptures together with sacred tradition as the supreme rule of faith, and will ever do so" (*Dei Verbum*, no. 21).

What the apocryphal gospels are:

✠ Beginning in the second century (and so separated in time from the events narrated) there emerged other gospels, called "apocryphal" (like the Gospel of Thomas, of Philip, of Peter, of James . . .). They

- Rose in the context of theological currents judged to be heretical by the Church at the time (e.g., the Gnostic gospels)
- (Some) contain truths; others present fantastical exaggerations in comparison with the canonical Gospels and have a theatrical flair characteristic of a popular Christianity
- In many cases intend to fill in the gaps in the four Gospels concerning certain periods of the life of Jesus (especially of his first thirty years), making plenty of room for imagination and invention
- Demonstrate particular interest in the dazzling aspects of the miracles, in the childhood of Jesus, in the stories of the apostles not mentioned in the Acts of the Apostles
- In some cases do not even mention the Death and Resurrection of Christ

✠ For these reasons, unlike the four canonical Gospels, they were not recognized as inspired by the Church, which, as soon as they were written, rejected them as unreliable and even harmful.

✠ In spite of this, they have had a certain influence in tradition and iconography, for example, in the presence of the ox and the donkey in the Nativity scene, and the names of Mary's parents (Joachim and Anne), which come to us from the Gospel of James, the most famous of the apocryphal gospels. Other apocryphal texts have come to light recently, like the Gospel of Thomas.

✠ It is necessary to recall that the four authentic Gospels preceded the apocryphal gospels. The Gospel of John, which is the last of the four, was composed around AD 90-95, many decades before a few authors wrote apocryphal gospels.

Are there extra-biblical testimonies that confirm the content of the Gospels?

There are a number of these:

- The first is that of Pliny the Younger, who was the proconsul of Bithynia during the years AD 111-113, and in one of the epistles sent to Emperor Trajan wrote that the Christians were "accustomed to gathering before dawn and intoning in alternating choirs a hymn to Christ as if he were a god." So he confirms that they were convinced of the divinity of Christ.
- Suetonius (circa AD 120), in his work *The Twelve Caesars*, referring to an event that occurred around the year AD 50, states that Claudius "expelled from

Rome the Jews who at the instigation of Chrestus were a constant cause of disorder" (*Vita Claudii* XXIII, 4). Suetonius wrote "Chrestus" instead of "Christus" because he did not know the difference between Jews and Christians, and because of the resemblance between Chrestos, which was a very common Greek name, and Christus, which means "anointed," "Messiah." So in Rome there were Jewish Christians and, as it were, unconverted Jews who were arguing about Christ, and who could appear in the eyes of the Roman authorities as a cause of public disorder.

- Then there is the testimony of the Roman historian Tacitus (circa AD 117), who in his *Annals* tells the story of the fire that broke out in Rome in AD 64. Nero was accused of being responsible for it, and in an effort to "put an end to this rumor, invented culprits and subjected to elaborate punishments those whom the rabble, detesting them on account of their wickedness, called Christians." Tacitus also states that "the origin of this name was Christ, who under the reign of Tiberius had been condemned to the torment by the procurator Pontius Pilate; and although briefly quelled, this deadly superstition spread once again, not only through Judea, the epicenter of that plague, but also to Rome, where all that is vile and shameful comes from all directions and is held in honor" (*Annals*, XV, 44).

- Among the Jewish sources, special mention should be made of Flavius Josephus (first century AD), the

Mishnah (second century AD), and the Talmud (fifth century AD).

What are the criteria for interpreting the Gospels?

✠ Here are some criteria:

- Above all, one must "be attentive to what the human authors truly wanted to affirm, and to what God wanted to reveal to us by their words. In order to discover the sacred authors' intention, the reader must take into account the conditions of their time and culture, the literary genres in use at that time, and the modes of feeling, speaking and narrating then current" (*Catechism of the Catholic Church* [CCC], nos. 109-110).

- Since the Gospels are inspired, there is another principle of correct interpretation, no less important than the previous one, without which Scripture would remain a "dead letter": "Holy Scripture must be read and interpreted according to the same Spirit by whom it was written" (*Dei Verbum*, no. 12). Vatican Council II indicates three criteria for an interpretation of Scripture in keeping with the Spirit who inspired it: (1) attention to the content and to the unity of the whole of Scripture; (2) interpretation of Scripture in the living Tradition of the Church; (3) respect for the analogy of faith, meaning the cohesion of the truths of faith with each other.

■ The Gospels must be interpreted under the guidance of the Magisterium of the Church, which is responsible for the authentic interpretation of the deposit of faith. "Sacred Scripture is written in the heart of the Church before it is on material instruments" (Origen, *Homiliae in Leviticum*, 5,5). "All of what has been said about the way of interpreting Scripture is subject finally to the judgment of the Church, which carries out the divine commission and ministry of guarding and interpreting the word of God" (*Dei Verbum*, no. 12). "The task of giving an authentic interpretation of the deposit of faith has been entrusted to the living teaching office of the Church alone, that is, to the successor of Peter, the Bishop of Rome, and to the bishops in communion with him. To this Magisterium, which in the service of the Word of God enjoys the certain charism of truth, belongs also the task of defining dogmas which are formulations of the truths contained in divine Revelation. This authority of the Magisterium also extends to those truths necessarily connected with Revelation" (*Compendium of the CCC*, no. 16).

■ The Gospels must be interpreted while keeping in mind the overall unity of the divine plan, which is realized in history (in terms of continuity, discontinuity, and progression), and that God has revealed in a full and definitive manner in his Only-Begotten Son, Jesus Christ. "All of divine Scripture is just one book, and this one book is Christ" (Hugh of Saint Victor, *De Arca Noe*, II, 8).

✠ "Sacred Scripture is the Word of God in human words. This means that every text must be read and interpreted keeping in mind the unity of the whole of Scripture, the living tradition of the Church and the light of the faith. If it is true that the Bible is also a literary work, even the great codex of universal culture, it is also true that it should not be stripped of the divine element but must be read in the same Spirit in which it was composed. Scientific exegesis and *lectio divina* are therefore both necessary and complementary in order to seek, through the literal meaning, the spiritual meaning that God wants to communicate to us today" (Benedict XVI, *Angelus*, October 26, 2008).

How should the Gospels be read?

✠ In the first place, a Gospel citation should be read as follows: Mt 3:1-4 means Matthew, chapter 3, verses 1 through 4.

✠ The reading of the Gospels can be done individually or in community, covering one or more passages, one or more pages. This reading must be done attentively, without skimming over what seems secondary, interpreting correctly the meaning of the biblical text. And it is developed, with the help of the Spirit, in meditation, contemplation, and prayer.

- *Meditation* (*Meditatio*): What has been read must be compared with parallel biblical passages and applied to personal life, making a concrete commitment.

- *Contemplation* (*Contemplatio*): This is the moment of reflection, of silence, and of adoration, until becoming aware of the living presence of God.
- *Prayer* (*Oratio*): This is the moment of praise and intercession. The disciple shares his or her faith with others and prays according to what the encounter with God in that passage of Scripture has suggested. All of this can also take place in the context of a tranquil community celebration. "Prayer should accompany the reading of sacred Scripture, so that God and man may talk together" (*Dei Verbum*, no. 25).

✠ It is also necessary to keep a few prerequisites in mind in order to read the Gospels well:

- An understanding of the language of the Gospels and attention to the literal meaning, identifying also the aim, topic, and disposition of the text. This makes it necessary to have access to resources for correct exegesis, in order to avoid falling into arbitrary interpretations.
- Incessant reading and rereading of the Gospel texts in order to acquire a certain familiarity with their larger contours. In this regard it is helpful to compare one passage with other texts of the Bible. The unity of Sacred Scripture, which represents the unity of the plan of salvation, requires that an individual passage be read in the context of others, compared with others; that the Old Testament be read in the light of the New, but also that the New Testament

be read in the light of the Old, in order to recognize the "pedagogy of God," because the New Testament cannot be understood outside of its close relationship with the Old Testament and with the Jewish tradition that transmitted it.

- Contemporary application. It is necessary to apply the biblical text to our own time. Through a reading of the past, the Spirit helps us to discern the meaning that he himself is giving to the problems and events of our time, allowing us to read the Bible in light of life, and life in light of the Bible.
- Attention to the meanings of Sacred Scripture, and therefore of the Gospels

What are the meanings of Sacred Scripture?

"According to an ancient tradition, one can distinguish between two *senses* of Scripture: the literal and the spiritual, the latter being subdivided into the allegorical, moral and anagogical senses. The profound concordance of the four senses guarantees all its richness to the living reading of Scripture in the Church.

"The *literal sense* is the meaning conveyed by the words of Scripture and discovered by exegesis, following the rules of sound interpretation: 'All other senses of Sacred Scripture are based on the literal.'

"The *spiritual sense*. Thanks to the unity of God's plan, not only the text of Scripture but also the realities and events about which it speaks can be signs.

"The *allegorical sense*. We can acquire a more profound understanding of events by recognizing their significance in Christ; thus the crossing of the Red Sea is a sign or type of Christ's victory and also of Christian Baptism.

"The *moral sense*. The events reported in Scripture ought to lead us to act justly. As St. Paul says, they were written 'for our instruction.'

"The *anagogical sense* (Greek: *anagoge*, 'leading'). We can view realities and events in terms of their eternal significance, leading us toward our true homeland: thus the Church on earth is a sign of the heavenly Jerusalem.

"A medieval couplet summarizes the significance of the four senses: 'The Letter speaks of deeds; Allegory to faith; the Moral how to act; Anagogy our destiny' (*Littera gesta docet, quid credas allegoria. Moralis quid agas, quo tendas anagogia*)" (CCC, nos. 115-118).

✠

For more on this topic, see the following pontifical documents:

Vatican Council II, *Dei Verbum*
Catechism of the Catholic Church, nos. 74-141
Compendium of the CCC, nos. 11-24

IV
Jesus Christ: True God and True Man

In what way is Jesus Christ true God and true Man?

He is so in a unique and singular way.

✠ The Catholic faith forcefully emphasizes the uniqueness of the wonderful union of the divine nature and the human nature in the one divine Person of the Word: "The unique and altogether singular event of the Incarnation of the Son of God does not mean that Jesus Christ is part God and part man, nor does it imply that he is the result of a confused mixture of the divine and the human. He became truly man while remaining truly God. Jesus Christ is true God and true man. During the first centuries, the Church had to defend and clarify this truth of faith against the heresies that falsified it" (CCC, no. 464).

✠ Here is how the Council of Chalcedon (451) expressed this truth: Jesus Christ is "one selfsame Son, our Lord Jesus Christ, perfect in his divinity and perfect in his humanity; true God and true man, composed of rational soul and body; consubstantial with the Father as for divinity, consubstantial with us as for humanity, 'like us in all things, except for sin' (Heb 4:15); generated by the Father before all ages according to the divinity, and in these last times, for us and for our salvation, born of the Virgin Mary and Mother of God, according to the humanity."

✠ Even the names used to refer to Jesus Christ emphasize his divine-human dimension:

- "Jesus" means "God saves" humanity and the universe.
- "Christ" means "anointed," the Messiah whom "God anointed . . . with the holy Spirit and power" (Acts 10:38) and "the one who is to come" (Lk 7:14) into the world.
- "Son of God" expresses the filial, characteristic, unique, and eternal relationship of Christ with God his Father.
- "Lord" indicates his divine sovereignty over humanity and the universe (see CCC, nos. 430-455).

How does this mysterious union take place in the Incarnation?

"Christ's human nature belongs, as his own, to the divine person of the Son of God, who assumed it. Everything that Christ is and does in this nature derives from 'one of the Trinity.' The Son of God therefore communicates to his humanity his own personal mode of existence in the Trinity. In his soul as in his Body, Christ thus expresses humanly the divine ways of the Trinity" (CCC, no. 470).

His Body is therefore a true human body, through which, "though invisible in his own divine nature, he has appeared visibly in ours" (Preface II of the Nativity of the Lord, *The Roman Missal*). "The Son of God . . . worked with human hands, He thought with a human mind, acted by human choice, and loved with a human heart. Born of the Virgin Mary, He has truly been made one of us, like us in all things except sin" (*Gaudium et Spes*, no. 22).

How are knowledge and will realized in Jesus Christ as God and Man?

"This truly human knowledge of God's Son expressed the divine life of his person" (CCC, no. 473). "The Son of God knew everything; and this by means of the same man that he had taken on; not by the (human) nature, but because of the fact that this was united to the Word" (St. Maximus the Confessor, *Quaestiones et Dubia*, Q. I, 67). At the same time, "Jesus had a divine will and a human will. In his earthly life the Son of God humanly willed all that he had divinely decided with the Father and the Holy Spirit for our salvation. The human will of Christ followed without opposition or reluctance the divine will or, in other words, it was subject to it" (*Compendium of the* CCC, no. 91).

Is the maternity of the Virgin Mary also a sign of this wonderful divine-human union of Christ?

Certainly.

"The One whom she conceived as man by the Holy Spirit, who truly became her Son according to the flesh, was none other than the Father's eternal Son, the second person of the Holy Trinity. Hence the Church confesses that Mary is truly 'Mother of God'" (CCC, no. 495).

This is also the significance of the virginal conception of Jesus in the womb of the Blessed Mother: "Jesus was conceived in the womb of the Virgin solely by the power of the Holy Spirit without the intervention of a man. He is the Son of the heavenly Father according to his divine nature and the Son of Mary according to his human nature. He is, however, truly the Son of God in both natures since there is in him only one Person who is divine" (*Compendium of the* CCC, no. 98).

How does the Paschal Mystery of Christ highlight the wonderful unity of his being true God and true man?

✠   If the Son of God was able to suffer, to be crucified, to die, to be buried . . . it is because he is true man.

On the other hand, if his Death was able to have a redemptive, salvific, justifying value for all human beings, and above all if his Resurrection was able to take place, it is because he is truly Son of God.

✠ The very accusation that some of the leaders of Israel made against Jesus, and because of which he was handed over to Pilate to be condemned to death, is that he, a human being like the others, dared to proclaim himself Son of God, he addressed God as his Father, he attributed to himself prerogatives that belong only to God. "Jesus gave scandal above all when he identified his merciful conduct toward sinners with God's own attitude toward them. He went so far as to hint that by sharing the table of sinners he was admitting them to the messianic banquet. But it was most especially by forgiving sins that Jesus placed the religious authorities of Israel on the horns of a dilemma. Were they not entitled to demand in consternation, 'Who can forgive sins but God alone?' By forgiving sins Jesus either is blaspheming as a man who made himself God's equal, or is speaking the truth and his person really does make present and reveal God's name" (CCC, no. 589).

✠ "His suffering and death showed how his humanity was the free and perfect instrument of that divine love which desires the salvation of all people. . . . The human will of the Son of God remained faithful to the will of the Father for our salvation. Jesus accepted the duty to carry our sins in his Body 'becoming obedient to death' (Phil 2:8). . . . Jesus freely offered his life as an expiatory sacrifice, that is, he made reparation for our sins with the full obedience of his love unto death. This love 'to the end' (Jn 13:1) of the Son of God reconciled all of humanity with the Father. The paschal sacrifice of Christ, therefore, redeems humanity in a way that is unique, perfect, and definitive; and it opens up for them communion with God" (*Compendium of the* CCC, nos. 119, 121, 122).

✠ The Resurrection of Christ highlights his being God and man, under four aspects:

- "The Resurrection, insofar as it is the entrance of Christ's humanity into the glory of God, transcends and surpasses history as a mystery of faith" (*Compendium of the* CCC, no. 128).
- "His risen body is that which was crucified and bears the marks of his passion. However it also participates in the divine life, with the characteristics of a glorified body" (*Compendium of the* CCC, no. 129).
- "The Resurrection of Christ is a transcendent work of God. The three Persons act together according to what is proper to them: the Father manifests his power; the Son 'takes again' the life which he freely offered (Jn 10:17), reuniting his soul and his body which the Spirit brings to life and glorifies" (*Compendium of the* CCC, no. 130).
- "The Resurrection is the climax of the Incarnation. It confirms the divinity of Christ and all the things which he did and taught. It fulfills all the divine promises made for us" (*Compendium of the* CCC, no. 131).

Thus "the truth of Jesus' divinity is confirmed by his Resurrection. He had said: 'When you have lifted up the Son of Man, then you will know that I am he' (Jn 8:28). The Resurrection of the crucified one shows that he was truly 'I Am,' the Son of God and God himself. So St. Paul could declare to the Jews: 'What God promised to the fathers, this he has fulfilled to us their children by raising Jesus; as also it is written in the second psalm, "You are my son, today I have begotten you."'" (CCC, no. 653).

✠ His Ascension into heaven itself "stays closely linked to the first, that is, to his descent from heaven in the Incarnation. Only the one who 'came from the Father' can return to the Father: Christ Jesus. 'No one has ascended into heaven but he who descended from heaven, the Son of Man.' Left to its own natural powers humanity does not have access to the 'Father's house,' to God's life and happiness. Only Christ can open to man such access that we, his members, might have confidence that we too shall go where he, our Head and our Source, has preceded us" (CCC, no. 661).

In what sense does the Church, in being visible and spiritual at the same time, find its justification in the fact that its founder is true God and true man?

✠ "'The one mediator, Christ, established and ever sustains here on earth his holy Church, the community of faith, hope, and charity, as a visible organization through which he communicates truth and grace to all men.' The Church is at the same time:

- A 'society structured with hierarchical organs and the mystical body of Christ
- The visible society and the spiritual community

- The earthly Church and the Church endowed with heavenly riches.'

"These dimensions together constitute 'one complex reality which comes together from a human and a divine element.'

✠ "'The Church is essentially both human and divine, visible but endowed with invisible realities, zealous in action and dedicated to contemplation, present in the world, but as a pilgrim, so constituted that in her the human is directed toward and subordinated to the divine, the visible to the invisible, action to contemplation, and this present world to that city yet to come, the object of our quest'" (CCC, no. 771).

In what way is the wonderful union of the divine and human nature of Christ the basis of the entire sacramental economy of the Church?

✠ "'Seated at the right hand of the Father' and pouring out the Holy Spirit on his Body which is the Church, Christ now acts through the sacraments he instituted to communicate his grace. The sacraments are perceptible signs (words and actions) accessible to our human nature" (CCC, no. 1084). And the *Compendium of the CCC* quite rightly presents a beautiful quote from St. Leo the Great: "What was visible in our Savior has passed over into his mysteries" (no. 225).

✠ "A sacramental celebration is woven from signs and symbols. In keeping with the divine pedagogy of salvation, their meaning is rooted in the work of creation and in human culture, specified by the events of the Old Covenant and fully revealed in the person and work of Christ" (CCC, no. 1145).

✠ On the sacramental signs: "Some come from created things (light, water, fire, bread, wine, oil); others come from social life (washing, anointing, breaking of bread). Still others come from the history of salvation in the Old Covenant (the Passover rites, the sacrifices, the laying on of hands, the consecrations). These signs, some of which are normative and unchangeable, were taken up by Christ and are made the bearers of his saving and sanctifying action" (*Compendium of the CCC*, no. 237).

✠ Sacred images, which transcribe the message that Sacred Scripture transmits in words, exist in reference to Christ. In fact, "the image of Christ is the liturgical icon par excellence. Other images, representations of Our Lady and of the Saints, signify Christ who is glorified in them" (*Compendium of the CCC*, no. 240).

✠ "Liturgical catechesis aims to initiate people into the mystery of Christ (It is 'mystagogy.') by proceeding from the visible to the invisible, from the sign to the thing signified, from the 'sacraments' to the 'mysteries'" (CCC, no. 1075).

How is Christian moral life a life in Christ, God and man?

The *Catechism* highlights these truths in various ways.

✠ For example, it introduces the third part with the beautiful testimony of St. John Eudes: "I ask you to consider that our Lord Jesus Christ is your true head, and that you are one of his members. He belongs to you as the head belongs to its members; all that is his is yours: his spirit, his heart, his body and soul, and all his faculties. You must make use of all these as of your own, to serve, praise, love, and glorify God. You belong to him, as members belong to their head. And so he longs for you to use all that is in you, as if it were his own, for the service and glory of the Father" (*Tractatus de admirabili corde Jesu*, 1,5).

✠   In presenting the human person as the image of God, it immediately does so in relation to Christ, according to the guidelines of *Gaudium et Spes*: "'Christ . . . in the very revelation of the mystery of the Father and of his love, makes man fully manifest to himself and brings to light his exalted vocation.' It is in Christ, 'the image of the invisible God,' that man has been created 'in the image and likeness' of the Creator. It is in Christ, Redeemer and Savior, that the divine image, disfigured in man by the first sin, has been restored to its original beauty and ennobled by the grace of God" (CCC, no. 1701). And a few paragraphs later, it states: "He who believes in Christ becomes a son of God. This filial adoption transforms him by giving him the ability to follow the example of Christ. It makes him capable of acting rightly and doing good. In union with his Savior, the disciple attains the perfection of charity which is holiness. Having matured in grace, the moral life blossoms into eternal life in the glory of heaven" (CCC, no. 1709).

✠ The Beatitudes themselves, which show human beings the way to find the true and complete response to their innate desire for happiness, "depict the countenance of Jesus Christ and portray his charity. They express the vocation of the faithful associated with the glory of his Passion and Resurrection" (CCC, no. 1717).

✠ And also in presenting the Decalogue, which makes up the framework of the second section of its third part, the *Catechism* situates it in direct relationship with Jesus Christ: "To follow Jesus involves keeping the commandments. The law has not been abolished but man is invited to rediscover it in the Person of the divine Master who realized it perfectly in himself, revealed its full meaning and attested to its permanent validity" (*Compendium of the* CCC, no. 434).

Christ is therefore the one who, during his earthly life as a member of humanity, was able—precisely by virtue of his special and unique authority as Son of God—both to confirm the Ancient Law and to give it its correct and complete interpretation and implementation.

Does Christian prayer itself find its foundation in the fact that Jesus Christ is God and man?

Of course. In fact:

✠ Christian prayer is above all "a covenant relationship between God and man in Christ. It is the action of God and of man, springing forth from both the Holy Spirit and ourselves, wholly directed to the Father, in union with the human will of the Son of God made man" (CCC, no. 2564).

Moreover, "the drama of prayer is fully revealed to us in the Word who became flesh and dwells among us. To seek to understand his prayer through what his witnesses proclaim to us in the Gospel is to approach the holy Lord Jesus as Moses approached the burning bush: first to contemplate him in prayer, then to hear how he teaches us to pray, in order to know how he hears our prayer" (CCC, no. 2598).

✠ In this way, Christian prayer is fully revealed and realized in Christ, who, "with his human heart, learned how to pray from his mother and from the Jewish tradition. But his prayer sprang from a more secret source because he is the eternal Son of God who in his holy humanity offers his perfect filial prayer to his Father" (*Compendium of the* CCC, no. 541).

✠ Even the preeminent prayer of the Church, the Our Father, the Lord's Prayer, is called this because it was taught to us by the Lord Jesus himself.

"The prayer that comes to us from Jesus is truly unique: it is 'of the Lord.' On the one hand, in the words of this prayer the only Son gives us the words the Father gave him: he is the master of our prayer. On the other, as Word incarnate, he knows in his human heart the needs of his human brothers and sisters and reveals them to us: he is the model of our prayer" (CCC, no. 2765).

For more on this topic, see:

Vatican Council II, *Lumen Gentium*; *Gaudium et Spes*
Catechism of the Catholic Church
Compendium of the CCC

V
The Resurrection of Christ

What is the importance of the Resurrection of Christ?

The Resurrection of Christ is the extraordinary, original, unrepeatable, singular event in human history. It is the central reality of Christianity and of Christian testimony, from the beginning until the end of time. It is the source and synthesis of all Christian preaching and Christian hope; it confers meaning on the entire liturgy, on our Eucharist, the source and summit of the Church's entire life.

Easter is the principal and most important feast of the whole year, "the foundation and nucleus of the whole liturgical year" (*Sacrosanctum Concilium*, no. 106).

We will try to illustrate briefly this extraordinary importance of the Resurrection of Christ, starting with its historicity.

A. The Historicity of the Resurrection of Christ

In what sense is the Resurrection of Christ a historical event?

✠ It is not so in the sense that anyone could have witnessed it directly, photographing it at the moment it took place. "O truly blessed night," we sing in the *Exsultet* of the Easter Vigil, "which alone deserved to know the time and the hour when Christ rose from the realm of the dead! . . .

"No one was an eyewitness to Christ's Resurrection and no evangelist describes it. No one can say how it came about physically. Still less was its innermost essence, his passing over to another life, perceptible to the senses" (CCC, no. 647).

✠ Nonetheless, the Resurrection of Christ is a historical event in the sense that it really took place in history and had historically attested signs and testimonies.

✠ At the same time, it is also a mysterious event, which transcends and exceeds history itself, in that it is a mystery of faith, and as such, it requires faith, a gift from God, by virtue of which one can exclaim with St. Thomas before the Risen Christ: "My Lord and my God!" (Jn 20:28).

✠ Therefore, the Resurrection of Christ "is not a theory, but a historical reality revealed by the man Jesus Christ by means of his 'Passover' . . . It is neither a myth nor a dream, it is not a vision or a utopia, it is not a fairy tale, but it is a singular and unrepeatable event" (Pope Benedict XVI, *Urbi et Orbi* message, 2009).

✠ St. Paul says that Christ "was raised on the third day in accordance with the scriptures" (1 Cor 15:4). "Many exegetes see the words: 'he was raised on the third day in accordance with the Scriptures' as an important reference to what we read in Psalm 16[15] in which the Psalmist proclaims: 'Because you will not abandon my soul to the nether world, nor will you suffer your faithful one to undergo corruption' (ibid., v. 10). This is one of the texts of the Old Testament, cited frequently in early Christianity to prove Jesus' messianic character. Since according to the Jewish interpretation corruption began after the third day, the words of Scripture are fulfilled in Jesus who rose on the third day, that is, before corruption began" (Pope Benedict XVI, General audience, April 15, 2009).

What are the signs, the proofs, that attest to the Resurrection of Christ?

✠ There are two of them in particular:

- The empty tomb
- The appearances of the Risen Christ

✠ Thanks to these proofs, the historical truth of the Resurrection of Christ "is amply documented even if today, as in the past, there are many who in various ways cast doubt on it or even deny it" (Pope Benedict XVI, General audience, March 26, 2008).

What is the value of the empty tomb?

"The first element we encounter in the framework of the Easter events is the empty tomb. In itself it is not a direct proof of Resurrection; the absence of Christ's body from the tomb could be explained otherwise. Nonetheless the empty tomb was still an essential sign for all. Its discovery by the disciples was the first step toward recognizing the very fact of the Resurrection. This was the case, first with the holy women, and then with Peter. The disciple 'whom Jesus loved' affirmed that when he entered the empty tomb and discovered 'the linen cloths lying there,' 'he saw and believed.' This suggests that he realized from the empty tomb's condition that the absence of Jesus' body could not have been of human doing and that Jesus had not simply returned to earthly life as had been the case with Lazarus" (CCC, no. 640).

What are the characteristics of the appearances of the Risen Christ?

✠ These appearances

- Are rigorously documented by the New Testament (the Gospels, the Acts of the Apostles, and the Apostolic Letters agree in their descriptions of them)
- Are numerous: to the two Marys (Mt 28:1-8); to Mary Magdalene (Jn 20:11-18); to the disciples in the upper room (Jn 20:19-23); to the disciples on the road to Emmaus (Lk 24:13-35; Mk 16:12-13); to Thomas (Jn 20:24-29); to the disciples at the Sea of

Tiberias (Jn 21:1-14); to others (Jn 20:30-31); to Paul and the "five hundred brothers" (1 Cor 15:3-9; 20-21)

- Manifest a fundamental reality: the initiative is not that of the disciples, but of Christ, the Living One, as the book of Acts also attests: "He presented himself alive to them" (1:3). So they are not something that originates from the disciples, but from Christ himself.

- Show that the risen Body of Jesus is the same one that was tortured and crucified, because it still bears the marks of the Passion (see Jn 20:20, 27)

- Attest to the new dimension of the Risen One, his mode of being "according to the Spirit," which is new and different with respect to the previous mode of existence, "according to the flesh"

- Allow the Risen Jesus to entrust the apostles and disciples with the mission of proclaiming to others his Resurrection and his Gospel: "Go, therefore, and make disciples of all nations, baptizing them in the name of the Father, and of the Son, and of the holy Spirit" (Mt 28:19); "He said to them, 'Go into the whole world and proclaim the gospel to every creature'" (Mk 16:15).

✠ The Risen Jesus appears first of all to women, who were therefore the first to encounter the Risen Jesus and to tell the news to the apostles:

- Incredulous women, who because of this, on Easter morning, are also admonished by the angel: "Why do you seek the living one among the dead?" (Lk 24:5).

- "Unreliable" women: at the time, in the context of Judaism, the testimony of women had no official or legal value.

Now the fact that Jesus manifested himself to women first is further evidence for belief in the historical truth of his Resurrection and of the veracity of the Gospel accounts. In fact, if it had been made up, why would someone put the important testimony of the Resurrection of Christ in the mouths of women, whose words had no legal value whatsoever?

What value does the testimony of the apostles have?

✠ The value of the testimony of the apostles appears from the characteristics that this testimony presents:

- The core of the testimony of different persons, in different situations and places, is consistent in all of the appearances and attests that the Lord is risen and has shown himself alive.
- It is a very ancient testimony. The most ancient testimony of the Resurrection is the one given by the Apostle Paul: "For I handed on to you as of first importance what I also received: that Christ died for our sins in accordance with the scriptures; that he was buried; that he was raised on the third day in accordance with the scriptures; that he appeared to Cephas, then to the Twelve. After that, he appeared to more than five hundred brothers at once, most of whom are still living, though some have fallen asleep. After that he appeared to James, then to all

the apostles. Last of all, as to one born abnormally, he appeared to me" (1 Cor 15:3-8).

These words were written around AD 56 or 57. But St. Paul states that he received from others, after his conversion, the core of this testimony (see Acts 9:3-18). And therefore this text can be dated back to around AD 35, five or six years after the Death of Christ. This testimony is therefore of great historical value, because of its antiquity.

- The apostles appear as witness, not as inventors of this testimony. In fact, the Resurrection appeared to them as something impossible, beyond anything imaginable. Jesus himself must overcome their resistance, their incredulity: "How slow of heart to believe all that the prophets spoke!" (Lk 24:25); "Why are you troubled? And why do questions arise in your hearts? Look at my hands and my feet, that it is I myself. Touch me and see, because a ghost does not have flesh and bones as you can see I have" (Lk 24:38).

✠ From their testimony, it appears that the Resurrection of Christ is an event that

- Transcends them, who are nonetheless its witnesses. In this regard, we must not forget that when Jesus was captured and crucified, the disciples ran away and thought that it was all over for Jesus, harboring no hope of a resurrection. Instead of enthusiasm, after the Death of Christ the apostles felt nothing but disappointment and dismay. So the Resurrection was beyond their thoughts and expectations.

- Therefore surpasses, and indeed overturns, the thinking of the apostles, who could never have dreamed up such a story

- Changes their lives. It makes them so courageous as to face even martyrdom. This is more evidence in favor of the historicity of the Resurrection of Christ, in that no one dies for the sake of a lie.

B. THE IMPORTANCE OF THE RESURRECTION OF CHRIST

What importance did his Resurrection have for Christ?

The Resurrection of Christ

✠ Is not

- A purely spiritual, mental, or psychological event
- A return to earthly life, or the simple reanimation of a corpse, "as was the case with the raisings from the dead that he had performed before Easter: Jairus' daughter, the young man of Naim, Lazarus. These actions were miraculous events, but the persons miraculously raised returned by Jesus' power to ordinary earthly life. At some particular moment they would die again. Christ's Resurrection is essentially

different. In his risen body he passes from the state of death to another life beyond time and space. At Jesus' Resurrection his body is filled with the power of the Holy Spirit: he shares the divine life in his glorious state, so that St. Paul can say that Christ is 'the man of heaven'" (CCC, no. 646).

✠ But it is

- The culmination of his Incarnation
- The transformation of the Body of Christ, who is glorified and enters into a radically different order. His Body is different from how it was before. It is free from the laws of physics; it is no longer influenced by space and time. This is why he is able to come and go through closed doors; he appears and disappears where, how, and when he wishes. "His risen body is that which was crucified and bears the marks of his passion. However it also participates in the divine life, with the characteristics of a glorified body. Because of this the risen Jesus was utterly free to appear to his disciples how and where he wished and under various aspects" (*Compendium of the* CCC, no. 129).
- The work of all three Persons of the Trinity: "The Father manifests his power; the Son 'takes again' the life which he freely offered (Jn 10:17), reuniting his soul and his body which the Spirit brings to life and glorifies" (*Compendium of the* CCC, no. 130).

- The "yes" of God to Jesus, who has been condemned and killed by human beings: it is the seal that God stamps on the words and works of Jesus. It is the summit, the fullness, the synthesis of God's entire plan for his Son. The book of Acts attests: God "has provided confirmation for all by raising him from the dead" (17:31).
- The definitive and decisive proof of his divinity. He had said: "When you lift up the Son of Man, then you will realize that I AM" (Jn 8:28). The Death of Christ is the fulfillment of the immolation of the victim, the supreme testimony of his charity, while his Resurrection is the proof of his authenticity as Son of God and himself God. "The novelty of the Resurrection consists in the fact that Jesus, raised from the lowliness of his earthly existence, is constituted Son of God 'in power.' . . . The Resurrection thus reveals definitively the real identity and the extraordinary stature of the Crucified One. An incomparable and towering dignity: Jesus is God! For St. Paul, the secret identity of Jesus is revealed even more in the mystery of the Resurrection than in the Incarnation" (Pope Benedict XVI, General audience, November 5, 2008).
- The confirmation of everything that
  - The Old Testament had prophesied (see Lk 24:26-27, 44-48)
  - Jesus himself said, promised (see Mt 28:6; Mk 16:7; Lk 24:6-7), and did
- The victory over sin and death

- The glorification, exaltation, raising up of Jesus to the right hand of the Father. In this way, "he is the Lord who now in his humanity reigns in the everlasting glory of the Son of God and constantly intercedes for us before the Father. He sends us his Spirit and he gives us the hope of one day reaching the place he has prepared for us" (*Compendium of the* CCC, no. 132).

What importance does the Resurrection of Christ have for us?

✠ The Resurrection of Christ does not only concern the person and work of Jesus. It is an event of universal impact that affects all of human history and the fate of every person, capable of penetrating and profoundly changing human existence.

✠ In fact, the Resurrection of Christ

- Is the foundation, the center, the synthesis, the culmination of the Christian faith: "If Christ has not been raised, then empty [too] is our preaching; empty, too, your faith" (1 Cor 15:14). It is not, in fact, anything new to believe that Jesus died: even the pagans believe this, everyone believes it. But the truly new, original, amazing thing is to believe that he is risen.
- Is the victory over sin and death, because in dying, Jesus has destroyed death and in rising has restored us to life. "He has brought us from slavery to freedom, from sadness to joy, from mourning to celebration, from darkness to light, from slavery to redemption.

And so we say before him: Alleluia!" (Melito of Sardis, *Easter Homily*).

- "Brings about filial adoption so that men become Christ's brethren, as Jesus himself called his disciples after his Resurrection: 'Go tell my brethren' (Mt 28:10). We are brethren not by nature, but by the gift of grace, because that adoptive filiation gains us a real share in the life of the only Son, which was fully revealed in his Resurrection" (CCC, no. 654).

- Is the true source of the loving service of the Church, which seeks to alleviate the suffering of the poor and the weak, since love has shown itself to be stronger than death, stronger than evil. "Through Easter the tree of faith blooms, the baptismal font becomes fruitful, the night shines with new light, the gift of heaven comes down and the sacrament gives its heavenly nourishment" (unknown ancient author, *Homily on Easter*, Discourse 35, 6-9).

- Took place on Sunday—"the first day of the week" (Mk 16:2)—and this is the reason that for Christians, Sunday is
  - The feast day of the week (*dies Domini*)
  - The principal day of the community celebration of the Eucharist (Sunday obligation). At the Holy Mass, in fact, the memorial of the Passover of the Lord is celebrated.

- Makes Easter Sunday the most important feast of the whole year. All of the other feasts stem from it.

- Becomes our resurrection, in a threefold dimension:

- *Baptismal*: "You were buried with him in baptism, in which you were also raised with him through faith in the power of God, who raised him from the dead" (Col 2:12).
- *Moral*: Every day we must die to sin and rise to new life: "If then you were raised with Christ, seek what is above, where Christ is seated at the right hand of God. Think of what is above, not of what is on earth" (Col 3:1-2).
- *Eschatological*: "The one who raised Christ from the dead will give life to your mortal bodies also, through his Spirit that dwells in you" (Rom 8:11).

■ Consoles our affliction here on earth. As all creation groans and suffers as with the pains of labor, so too we groan as we await the redemption of our bodies, our redemption and resurrection (see Rom 8:18-23).

What is the relationship between the Resurrection of Christ and the resurrection of our bodies?

✠ The Resurrection of Christ is the efficient cause (source) and example (model) of our justification and resurrection, the principle and origin of the future resurrection of our bodies that will take place at the end of this world: "But now Christ has been raised from the dead, the firstfruits of those who have fallen asleep . . . For just as in Adam all die, so too in Christ shall all be brought to life" (1 Cor 15:20-22). Therefore, at the end of time our bodies

- Will rise transformed: "*How* the resurrection of the body will come about exceeds the possibilities of our imagination and understanding" (*Compendium of the CCC*, no. 205).
- Will receive the same retribution that the soul has received from the judgment of God at the moment of death: "Those who have done good deeds to the resurrection of life, but those who have done wicked deeds to the resurrection of condemnation" (Jn 5:29).

✠ The resurrection of our bodies will be accompanied by the transformation of all creation and of the universe, which, "freed from its bondage to decay, will share in the glory of Christ with the beginning of 'the new heavens' and a 'new earth' (2 Pt 3:13). Thus, the fullness of the Kingdom of God will come about, that is to say, the definitive realization of the salvific plan of God to 'unite all things in him, things in heaven and things on earth' (Eph 1:10). God will then be 'all in all' (1 Cor 15:28) in eternal life" (*Compendium of the CCC*, no. 216).

On what day is Easter celebrated?

There is a difference in this regard between the Christians of the West and those of the East.

This difference depends on the use, in the calculation of the date of Easter, of two different calendars: the Gregorian and the Julian, respectively.

Ideally all Christians will one day celebrate Easter on the same date, in part to offer a better witness to the world.

VI
Christ Yes, Church No?

Can Christ be separated from the Church, or the Church from Christ?

✠ Absolutely not. Nothing is more absurd than separating the Church from Christ. There is no division or opposition whatsoever between Christ and the Church. And this is so for various reasons:

- The Church is founded on the apostles, who were specifically chosen by Christ. They "are the most evident sign of Jesus' will regarding the existence and mission of his Church, the guarantee that between Christ and the Church there is no opposition" (Pope Benedict XVI, General audience, March 15, 2006). "He went up the mountain and summoned those whom he wanted and they came to him. He appointed twelve [whom he also named apostles] that they might be with him and he might send them forth to preach and to have authority to drive out demons" (Mk 3:13-16; see Mt 10:1-4; Lk 6:12-16).

The apostles therefore provide us with a connection that goes back to Jesus himself.

■ The Church is the Body of Christ, who is its Head (see Eph 5:3). The Head cannot be separated from the body, or vice versa: the result would be two distorted, decapitated realities. Christ "is the head of the body, the church" (Col 1:18). Christ and the Church form "the fullness of Christ: Head and members. What is the Head, and what are the members? Christ and the Church" (St. Augustine, *In Iohannis evangelium tractatus*, 21, 8). "Head and members are, so to speak, only one mystical person" (St. Thomas Aquinas, *Summa Theologiae*, III, q. 48, a. 2, ad 1). "As head and body form a single man, so the Son of the Virgin and his elect members constitute a single man and the one Son of man. According to Scripture, the whole and complete Christ is Head and Body, which means all of the members together are a single Body, which with its Head is the one Son of man, with the Son of God is the one Son of God, with God is himself one God. Therefore the whole Body with the Head is Son of man, Son of God, God. This is why it says in the Gospel: I desire, O Father, that as you and I are one, so also they may be one with us (see Jn 17:21). According to this famous Scripture text, neither is the Body without the Head, nor is the Head without the Body, nor is the whole Christ, Head and Body, without God" (Blessed Isaac, *Discourse* 42).

- If one were to separate Christ from the Church
  - The result would be a falsification of the mission of Christ himself, "an imaginary Jesus. We cannot have Jesus without the reality he created and in which he communicates himself. Between the Son of God made flesh and his Church there is a profound, unbreakable and mysterious continuity by which Christ is present today in his people" (General audience, March 15, 2006).
  - One would substantially distort the nature of the Church itself, which, separated from its founder and Head, would no longer be the same reality. The Church comes from Christ, it was born from his will, from his heart, from his Death and Resurrection, from the pouring out of his Spirit. "The Church has no other light than Christ's; according to a favorite image of the Church Fathers, the Church is like the moon, all its light reflected from the sun" (CCC, no. 748). So the Church does not live of itself and for itself, but of Christ, with him, for him, and for the mission entrusted to it by him: to proclaim his Gospel and communicate to humanity the salvation won by Christ.
- We are members of the Church, brothers and sisters of one another, precisely and solely by virtue of the fact that we are brothers and sisters of Christ. We form the Church, in that Christ unites us intimately with

himself. It is he who makes all of us one with each other. The more we are united with him, the more we will be united with each other. This is accomplished in particular through the Sacrament of Baptism, by virtue of which we are united with the Death and Resurrection of Christ, and through the sacrament of the Eucharist, through which, "truly partaking of the body of the Lord . . . we are taken up into communion with Him and with one another" (*Lumen Gentium*, no. 7).

- "If one does not have the Church as mother, neither can one have God as Father" (St. Cyprian, *De Ecclesiae Catholicae Unitate*, 6).

- "Where the Church is, there also is the Spirit of God; and where the Spirit of God is, there is the Church and every grace" (*Against the Heresies* III, 24, 1-2).

- The Church is the solid and stable criterion of the canonicity of Sacred Scripture.

- "The Son of God has taken on human nature in a union so intimate that it is the selfsame and identical Christ not only in himself, who is the firstborn of all creatures, but also in all of his saints. And just as one cannot separate the Head from the members, so the members cannot be separated from the Head" (Pope Leo the Great, Discourse 12 on the Passion, 3, 6, 7).

✠ The slogan "Jesus yes, Church no" is therefore completely unacceptable and incompatible with the will of Christians and with the very nature of the Church. "Be careful not to separate the head from the body; do not prevent Christ from existing completely . . . 'What God has joined together, no human being must separate.' 'This is a great mystery, but I speak in reference to Christ and the church' (Mt 19:6; Eph 5:32). So do not try to dismember the head from the body. Christ would no longer be complete. In fact, Christ is never whole without the Church, just as the Church is never whole without Christ. The whole and complete Christ is head and body together" (Blessed Isaac, Homily 13, Discourse 11).

Are Christ and the Church identical?

✠ No. They are not identical, in that

- What Christ is "by nature, the members are by participation; what he is, he is in completely, while they are only partially. Finally, what the Son of God is by generation, his members are by adoption, as is written: 'You received a spirit of adoption, through which we cry, "Abba, Father!"' (Rom 8:15)" (Blessed Isaac, Discourse 42).

- The Church has been instituted by Christ, its founder. The difference between the two is therefore the difference between Creator and creature.

- The Church is made up of sinners, but Christ is without sin. "In the Apostles' Creed we profess 'one Holy Church' (Credo . . . Ecclesiam), and not to believe in the Church, so as not to confuse God with his works and to attribute clearly to God's goodness all the gifts he has bestowed on his Church" (CCC, no. 750).

✠ Between Christ and the Church, therefore, there is absolutely no separation or opposition, but also no equation. There is "the distinction of the two within a personal relationship" (CCC, no. 796). It is this particular relationship with Christ that identifies and characterizes the nature and mission of the Church.

"What does the word Church mean?

"The word *Church* refers to the people whom God calls and gathers together from every part of the earth. They form the assembly of those who through faith and Baptism have become children of God, members of Christ, and temples of the Holy Spirit" (*Compendium of the CCC*, no. 147).

"Are there other names and images with which the Bible speaks about the Church?

"In Sacred Scripture we find many images which bring out various complementary aspects of the mystery of the Church. The Old Testament favors those images that are bound to the people of God. The New Testament offers images that are linked to Christ as the Head of this people which is his Body. Other images are drawn from pastoral life (sheepfold, flock, sheep), from agriculture (field, olive grove, vineyard), from construction (dwelling place, stone, temple), and from family life (spouse, mother, family)" (*Compendium of the CCC*, no. 148).

"What is the origin and the fulfillment of the Church?

"The Church finds her origin and fulfillment in the eternal plan of God. She was prepared for in the Old Covenant with the election of Israel, the sign of the future gathering of all the nations. Founded by the words and actions of Jesus Christ, fulfilled by his redeeming death and Resurrection, the Church has been manifested as the mystery of salvation by the outpouring of the Holy Spirit at Pentecost. She will be perfected in the glory of heaven as the assembly of all the redeemed of the earth" (*Compendium of the* CCC, no. 149).

"What is the mission of the Church?

"The mission of the Church is to proclaim and establish the Kingdom of God begun by Jesus Christ among all peoples. The Church constitutes on earth the seed and beginning of this salvific Kingdom" (*Compendium of the* CCC, no. 150).

"In what way is the Church a mystery?

"The Church is a mystery in as much as in her visible reality there is present and active a divine spiritual reality which can only be seen with the eyes of faith" (*Compendium of the* CCC, no. 151).

"What does it mean to say that the Church is the universal sacrament of salvation?

"This means that she is the sign and instrument both of the reconciliation and communion of all of humanity with God and of the unity of the entire human race" (*Compendium of the CCC*, no. 152).

"Why is the Church the 'people of God'?

"The Church is the 'people of God' because it pleased God to sanctify and save men not in isolation but by making them into one people gathered together by the unity of the Father and the Son and the Holy Spirit" (*Compendium of the CCC*, no. 153).

"What are the characteristics of the people of God?

"One becomes a member of this people through faith in Christ and Baptism. This people has for its origin God the Father; for its head Jesus Christ; for its hallmark the dignity and freedom of the sons of God; for its law the new commandment of love; for its mission to be the salt of the earth and the light of the world; and for its destiny the Kingdom of God, already begun on earth" (*Compendium of the CCC*, no. 154).

"Why is the Church called the 'Bride of Christ'?

"She is called the 'Bride of Christ' because the Lord himself called himself her 'Spouse' (Mk 2:19). The Lord has loved the Church and has joined her to himself in an everlasting covenant. He has given himself up for her in order to purify her with his blood and 'sanctify her' (Eph 5:26), making her the fruitful mother of all the children of God. While the term 'body' expresses the unity of the 'head' with the members, the term 'bride' emphasizes the distinction of the two in their personal relationship" (*Compendium of the CCC*, no. 158).

"Why is the Church called the temple of the Holy Spirit?

"She is so called because the Holy Spirit resides in the body which is the Church, in her Head and in her members. He also builds up the Church in charity by the Word of God, the sacraments, the virtues, and charisms" (*Compendium of the CCC*, no. 159).

What are the distinctive features of the Church?

✠ The Church is

- *One*, "because she has as her source and exemplar the unity of the Trinity of Persons in one God. As her Founder and Head, Jesus Christ re-established the unity of all people in one body. As her soul, the Holy Spirit unites all the faithful in communion with Christ. The Church has but one faith, one sacramental life, one apostolic succession, one common hope, and one and the same charity" (*Compendium of the CCC*, no. 161).

- *Holy*, "insofar as the Most Holy God is her author. Christ has given himself for her to sanctify her and make her a source of sanctification. The Holy Spirit gives her life with charity. In the Church one finds the fullness of the means of salvation. Holiness is the vocation of each of her members and the purpose of all her activities. The Church counts among her members the Virgin Mary and numerous Saints who are her models and intercessors. The holiness of the Church is the fountain of sanctification for her children who here on earth recognize themselves as sinners ever in need of conversion and purification" (*Compendium of the* CCC, no. 165).

- *Catholic*, "that is universal, insofar as Christ is present in her: 'Where there is Christ Jesus, there is the Catholic Church' (St. Ignatius of Antioch). The Church proclaims the fullness and the totality of the faith; she bears and administers the fullness of the means of salvation; she is sent out by Christ on a mission to the whole of the human race" (*Compendium of the* CCC, no. 166).

- *Apostolic* "in her *origin* because she has been built on 'the foundation of the Apostles' (Eph 2:20). She is apostolic in her *teaching* which is the same as that of the Apostles. She is apostolic by reason of her *structure* insofar as she is taught, sanctified, and guided until Christ returns by the Apostles through their successors who are the bishops in communion with the successor of Peter" (*Compendium of the* CCC, no. 174).

✠ "These four characteristics, inseparably linked with each other, indicate essential features of the Church and her mission. The Church does not possess them of herself; it is Christ who, through the Holy Spirit, makes his Church one, holy, catholic, and apostolic, and it is he who calls her to realize each of these qualities.

"Only faith can recognize that the Church possesses these properties from her divine source. But their historical manifestations are signs that also speak clearly to human reason" (CCC, nos. 811-812). "The Church," as Vatican Council I recalls, "because of its eminent sanctity . . . its catholic unity, its unshakeable stability, is a great and perennial motive of credibility and an irrefutable witness to its own divine mission" (*Dei Filius*, no. 3).

Why is the Church always in need of purification?

Because it is made up of sinners. All the members of the pilgrim Church here on earth, including its ministers, are sinners. They must recognize themselves as such, humbly accepting God's forgiveness and constantly eradicating sin in themselves and others. "While Christ, 'holy, innocent, undefiled' (Heb 7:26) knew nothing of sin (2 Cor 5:21), but came to expiate only the sins of the people (see Heb 2:17), the Church, embracing sinners in her bosom, is at the same time holy and always in need of being purified, and incessantly pursues the path of penance and renewal" (*Lumen Gentium*, no. 8).

Who belongs to the Catholic Church?

"All human beings in various ways belong to or are ordered to the Catholic unity of the people of God. Fully incorporated into the Catholic Church are those who, possessing the Spirit of Christ, are joined to the Church by the bonds of the profession of faith, the sacraments, ecclesiastical government and communion. The baptized who do not enjoy full Catholic unity are in a certain, although imperfect, communion with the Catholic Church" (*Compendium of the* CCC, no. 168).

"Why did Christ institute an ecclesiastical hierarchy?

✠ "Christ instituted an ecclesiastical hierarchy with the mission of feeding the people of God in his name and for this purpose gave it authority. The hierarchy is formed of sacred ministers: bishops, priests, and deacons" (*Compendium of the* CCC, no. 179), to whom Christ entrusted the mission of teaching, sanctifying, and ruling. They exercise this mission as "slaves of Christ" (see Rom 1:1), imitating Christ himself, "who, though he was in the form of God, did not regard equality with God something to be grasped. Rather, he emptied himself, taking the form of a slave, coming in human likeness; and found human in appearance, he humbled himself, becoming obedient to death, even death on a cross" (Phil 2:6-8).

✠ "The word hierarchy is generally said to mean 'sacred dominion,' yet the real meaning is not this, but rather 'sacred origin,' that is to say: this authority does not come from man himself, but it has its origins in the sacred, in the Sacrament; so it subjects the person in second place to the vocation, to the mystery of Christ; it makes of the individual a servant of Christ, and only as a servant of Christ can he govern and guide for Christ and with Christ. Therefore he who enters into the Sacred Order of the Sacrament, the 'hierarchy,' is not an autocrat but he enters into a new bond of obedience to Christ: he is tied to Christ in communion with the other members of the Sacred Order, the Priesthood. Nor can the Pope, reference point for all the Pastors and for the communion of the Church, do what he likes; on the contrary, the Pope is the custodian of obedience to Christ, to his word summed up in the 'regula fidei,' in the Creed of the Church, and must lead the way in obedience to Christ and to his Church. Thus hierarchy implies a triple bond: in the first place the bond with Christ and with the order given by Our Lord to his Church; then the bond with the other Pastors in the one communion of the Church; and lastly, the bond with the faithful who are entrusted to the individual, in the order of the Church.

"Therefore it is clear that communion and hierarchy are not contrary to each other, but they influence each other. Together they form one thing (hierarchical communion)" (Pope Benedict XVI, General audience, May 26, 2010).

"What is the meaning of the affirmation 'Outside the Church there is no salvation'?

"This means that all salvation comes from Christ, the Head, through the Church which is his body. Hence they cannot be saved who, knowing the Church as founded by Christ and necessary for salvation, would refuse to enter her or remain in her. At the same time, thanks to Christ and to his Church, those who through no fault of their own do not know the Gospel of Christ and his Church but sincerely seek God and, moved by grace, try to do his will as it is known through the dictates of conscience can attain eternal salvation" (*Compendium of the* CCC, no. 171).

Why must the Church proclaim the Gospel to the whole world?

"The Church must do so because Christ has given the command: 'Go therefore and make disciples of all nations, baptizing them in the name of the Father and of the Son and of the holy Spirit' (Mt 28:19). This missionary mandate of the Lord has its origin in the eternal love of God who has sent his Son and the Holy Spirit because he 'desires all men to be saved and to come to the knowledge of the truth' (1 Tm 2:4)" (*Compendium of the* CCC, no. 172).

How should we view the Church?

We should view the Church as indicated by Benedict XVI, who said in his homily at St. Patrick's Cathedral in New York, referring to the neo-Gothic stained windows:

"From the outside, those windows are dark, heavy, even dreary. But once one enters the church, they suddenly come alive; reflecting the light passing through them, they reveal all their splendor. Many writers—here in America we can think of Nathaniel Hawthorne—have used the image of stained glass to illustrate the mystery of the Church herself" (April 19, 2008).

In what way does Mary Most Holy invite us to love the Church?

✠ She invites us to love the Church because she is

- The Mother of Christ, founder and Bridegroom of the Church
- The Mother and model of the Church

✠ There is also a close and intimate relationship between Mary Most Holy and the Church:

In fact, just as Head and members are at the same time one son and many sons, so also Mary and the Church are one and many mothers, one and many virgins. Both mothers, both virgins, both conceive by the work of the Spirit without concupiscence, both give the Father sons without sin. Without any sin, Mary generated the Head for the body, and in the remission of all sin the Church gave birth to the body for the Head. Both are mothers of Christ, but neither generates the whole without the other.

So it is correct to say that in the divinely inspired Scriptures, what is said in general about the Virgin Mother Church is meant to apply individually to the Virgin Mother Mary; and what is said in a special way about the Virgin Mother Mary must be applied in general to the Virgin Mother Church; and what is said about either of the two can be applied equally to the other (Blessed Isaac of the Star, Abbot, Discourse 51).

For more on this topic, see the following pontifical documents:

Vatican Council II, *Lumen Gentium; Sacrosanctum Concilium*
Catechism of the Catholic Church, nos. 748-945
Compendium of the CCC, nos. 147-193

VII
Primacy of Peter

On what basis is the primacy of Peter, and therefore of the pope, founded?

It is based on the will of Christ himself.

Where does this will of Christ appear?

In the pages of the Gospels and in parts of the Acts of the Apostles there are "numerous indications" that manifest the will of Christ to give Peter special prominence within the college of the apostles. For example:

✠   He is the only apostle to whom Jesus gives a new name, Cephas, which means "Rock." The evangelist John writes in this regard: "Jesus looked at him and said, 'You are Simon the son of John; you will be called Cephas' (which is translated Peter)" (Jn 1:42).

Jesus was not in the habit of changing the names of his disciples. With the exception of the nickname "sons of thunder," applied in a specific situation to the sons of Zebedee (see

Mk 3:17) and never used after this, he never gave a new name to any of his disciples.

But he did with Simon, calling him Cephas, a name that was translated into Greek as *Petros*, and into Latin as *Petrus*. And it was translated precisely because it was not only a name, it was a "mandate" that *Petrus* received from the Lord. It must not be forgotten that in the Old Testament, a change of name generally preceded the entrusting of a mission (see Jn 17:5; 32:28 ff., etc.). The new name Petrus would return repeatedly in the Gospels and would end up replacing the original name, Simon.

✠ Other indications are:

- After Jesus, Peter is the figure who appears most frequently in the New Testament: he is mentioned 154 times by that name.
- The Gospels tell us that Peter is among the first four disciples of Nazareth (see Lk 5:1-11).
- In Capernaum, the Master goes to stay in the home of Peter (see Mk 1:29).
- When the crowd begins pressing in on him at the shore of the Lake of Gennesaret, of the two boats moored there, Jesus chooses that of Simon (see Lk 5:3), and so the barque of Peter becomes the throne of Jesus.
- When in specific circumstances Jesus takes only three disciples with him, Peter is always presented as the first of the group, as at the resurrection of the daughter of Jairus (see Mk 5:37; Lk 8:51), the Transfiguration

(see Mk 9:2; Mt 17:1; Lk 9:28), and finally during the agony in the Garden of Gethsemane (see Mk 14:33; Mt 16:37).

■ The collectors of the temple tax go to Peter, and the Master pays only for the two of them (see Mt 17:24-27).

■ Jesus washes Peter's feet first at the Last Supper (see Jn 13:6).

■ It is for Peter alone that Jesus prays that his own faith might not fail, and that he might then strengthen that of the other disciples (see Lk 22:30-31).

Is Peter aware of this special position?

✠ Yes. In fact:

■ He is often the one who, in the name of the others, asks for the explanation of a difficult parable (see Mt 15:15) or the exact meaning of a precept (see Mt 18:21) or the formal promise of recompense (see Mt 19:27).

■ He is the one who resolves the embarrassment of certain situations, intervening in the name of all. So when Jesus, saddened by the incomprehension of the crowd after the discourse on the "bread of life," asks, "Do you also want to leave?" Peter's answer is simple: "Master, to whom shall we go? You have the words of eternal life" (see Jn 6:67-69).

■ Just as decisive is the profession of faith that he makes, again in the name of the Twelve, in the region of Caesarea Philippi. When Jesus asks him, "Who do you say that I am?," Peter responds, "You are the Messiah, the Son of the living God" (Mt 16:15-16).

✠ Peter followed Jesus with vigor, he passed the test of faith, abandoning himself to him. The moment nonetheless came in which he too gave in to fear and fell: he betrayed the Master (see Mk 14:66-72). Peter, who had professed absolute faith, knew the bitterness and humiliation of denial. But he repented, recognizing his grave sin: he burst into tears of repentance.

✠ And it is precisely to him, Peter, that Jesus entrusted a special mission, which is described by the evangelist John in the famous dialogue that took place between Jesus and Peter (see Jn 21:15-18). The dialogue features a very significant play on words. In Greek, the verb *filéo* expresses the love of friendship, tender but not absolute, while the verb *agapáo* (*agapé*) means love without reservation, total and unconditional. Jesus asks Peter the first time: "Simon . . . do you love me?" (*agapâs-me*), meaning this total and unconditional love (see Jn 21:15). Before the experience of betrayal, the apostle certainly would have said, "I love you (*agapô-se*) unconditionally." Now that he has known the bitter sadness of infidelity, the drama of his own weakness, he says with humility, "Lord, I love you (*filô-se*)," meaning "I love you with my poor human love." Christ insists: "Simon, do you love me with this total love that I want?" And Peter repeats the response of his humble human love: "*Kyries, filô-se.*" "Lord, I love you as I know how to love." The third time, Jesus asks Simon only, "*Fileîs-me?*," "Do you care for me?"

Simon understands that his poor love, the only kind he can offer, is enough for Jesus, but he is still saddened that the Lord had to ask this way. So he answers, "Lord, you know everything, you know that I love you (*filô-se*)."

What is the solemn declaration that defines, once and for all, the role of Peter in the Church?

✠ It is when Jesus affirms, "And so I say to you, you are Peter, and upon this rock I will build my church . . . I will give you the keys to the kingdom of heaven. Whatever you bind on earth shall be bound in heaven; and whatever you loose on earth shall be loosed in heaven" (Mt 16:18-19).

✠ In this affirmation, the three metaphors used by Jesus are very clear:

- Peter will be the rocky foundation on which the edifice of the Church will stand.
- He will have the keys of the Kingdom of Heaven, to open or close as he sees fit.
- Finally, he will be able to bind or loose, in the sense of establishing or prohibiting what he believes to be necessary for the life of the Church, which is the rest of Christ. It is still the Church of Christ, and not of Peter.
- This is the crystal-clear description of what the following reflection will refer to with the term "primacy of jurisdiction."

Is this position of preeminence that Jesus intended to confer on Peter still seen after the Resurrection of Christ?

✠ Of course. In fact:

- Jesus tells the women to take the news to Peter, separately from the other apostles (see Mk 16:7).
- Mary Magdalene runs to him and to John to tell them that the stone had been rolled back from the entrance to the tomb (see Jn 20:2), and John stands aside for him when the two arrive at the empty tomb (see Jn 20:4-6).
- Peter is the first apostle to witness an appearance of the Risen One (see Lk 24:34; 1 Cor 15:5).

✠ This role, emphasized decisively (see Jn 20:3-10), marks the continuity between the preeminence he has within the group of apostles and the preeminence that he will continue to have in the community that emerges with the events of Easter, as attested to in the book of Acts (see Acts 1:15-26; 2:14-40; 3:12-26; 4:8-12; 5:1-11, 29; 8:14-17; 10, etc.).

✠ His conduct is considered so decisive as to be at the center of observations, and also of criticisms (see Acts 11:1-18; Gal 2:11-14).

✠ At the Council of Jerusalem, Peter plays an important executive role (see Acts 15 and Gal 2:1-10), and precisely because of the fact that he is the authentic witness of the faith, Paul himself would recognize in him a certain quality of "primacy" (see 1 Cor 15:5; Gal 1:18; 2:7; etc.).

✠ Moreover, the fact that various key texts referring to Peter can be traced back to the context of the Last Supper, at which Christ confirms upon Peter the ministry of strengthening his brothers (see Lk 22:31f.), shows how the Church that is born from the Passover memorial, celebrated in the Eucharist, has one of its constitutive elements in the ministry entrusted to Peter.

What is the ultimate meaning of the primacy of Peter?

✠ This contextualization of the primacy of Peter at the Last Supper, at the moment of the institution of the Eucharist, the Passover of the Lord, also indicates the ultimate meaning of this primacy:

- Peter, for all time, must be the custodian of communion with Christ; he must guide people to communion with Christ.
- He must take care that the net not be broken, so that universal communion may endure. Only when we are united with Peter can we be united with Christ, who is the Lord of all.

✠ Peter's responsibility is to guarantee communion with Christ through the charity of Christ, guiding people to the realization of this charity in everyday life. "The Petrine Primacy has this mandate to make unity visible and concrete in the historical, concrete multiplicity, in the unity of present, past, future and eternity" (Pope Benedict XVI, Address, July 29, 2010).

✠ Peter's role has priorities. "The first priority for the Successor of Peter was laid down by the Lord in the Upper Room in the clearest of terms: 'You . . . strengthen your brothers' (Lk 22:32). Peter himself formulated this priority anew in his first Letter: 'Always be prepared to make a defense to anyone who calls you to account for the hope that is in you' (1 Pt 3:15)" (Pope Benedict XVI, Letter to the Bishops, March 10, 2009).

In what way is the primacy of Peter connected to Rome?

✠ Peter went to Rome, the center of the Empire, symbol of the "Orbis"—the "Urbs" that expresses the "Orbis," the earth—where he concluded his service to the Gospel with martyrdom. This is why the See of Rome, which had received the greater honor, also received the duty entrusted to Peter by Christ: to be at the service of all the particular Churches for the edification and unity of the whole People of God.

✠ The See of Rome was thus recognized as that of the successor of Peter, and the *cathedra* of its bishop represented that of the apostle whom Christ had charged with feeding his whole flock.

This is attested to by the most ancient Fathers of the Church, for example:

- St. Irenaeus (bishop of Lyons until 202, but originally from Asia Minor), who in his treatise *Against the Heresies* in AD 180, described the Church of Rome as the "greatest and most ancient, known to all . . . founded and constituted in Rome by the two most glorious apostles Peter and Paul," and added, "This Church, because of its eminent superiority, must be given the agreement of the universal Church, meaning the faithful everywhere" (III, 3, 2-3).

- Tertullian affirmed a short time later (in AD 200), "This Church of Rome, how blessed it is! It was the apostles themselves who poured out for it, with their blood, doctrine whole and entire" (*The Prescription of the Heretics*, 36).

- St. Jerome (who was born around 340 in Stridon, on the border of Pannonia): "I decided to consult the throne of Peter, where the faith exalted by the mouth of an apostle is found; I now come to ask for nourishment for my soul there, where I once received the garment of Christ. I follow no primacy other than that of Christ; for this reason I put myself in communion with all blessedness, with the throne of Peter. I know that the Church is built on this rock" (*Letters*, I, 15, 1-2).

- There is also the important letter that St. Clement (the third successor of Peter) sent, in 96, to the Church of Corinth. This letter constitutes a first exercise of the Roman primacy after the death of St. Peter. With regard to this letter, St. Irenaeus writes, "Under Clement, when a serious disagreement broke out among the brothers of Corinth, the Church of Rome sent to the Corinthians an extremely important letter to reconcile them in peace, to renew their faith and proclaim the tradition that it had received from the apostles a short time before" (*Adversus Haereses* 3, 3, 3).

✠ As for the relationship between Peter and his successors, it must be said that "many prerogatives were exclusive to his person, and on the other hand, nothing was transmitted to his successors that was not already found in him" (St. Leo the Great, *Discourse* 4, 1-2).

What can we do for the pope?

We can and must pray that the primacy of Peter, entrusted to poor human persons, may always be exercised in this original sense willed by the Lord and thus may always be recognized in its true significance by our brothers and sisters not yet in full communion with the Catholic Church.

For more on this topic, read:

Benedict XVI, General audiences, May 17-24 and June 7, 2006

VIII
Ecumenism

What is ecumenism?

✠ This is the movement that strives for the unity of Christians and includes "those activities and enterprises which, according to various needs of the Church and opportune occasions, are started and organized for the fostering of unity among Christians" (*Unitatis Redintegratio*, no. 4).

The search for Christian unity is an increasingly urgent task for the Catholic Church. Ecumenism—as distinguished from interreligious dialogue—finds its foundation in the testament left to us by Jesus himself on the eve of his death: "*Ut unum sint*" (Jn 17:21). Vatican Council II described the effort for Christian unity as one of its main goals (*Unitatis Redintegratio*, no. 1) and as an impulse of the Holy Spirit (*Unitatis Redintegratio*, nos. 1, 4). Pope John Paul II repeatedly emphasized that "the Catholic Church committed herself irrevocably to following the path of the ecumenical venture" (*Ut Unum Sint*, no. 3). And the Holy Father Benedict XVI, from the first days of his pontificate, has pledged that he is fully committed to the restoration of the full and visible unity of all the followers of Christ. In this task, the primary criterion is the unity of the faith.

The point of departure for ecumenism is Baptism; the point of arrival is the shared celebration of the Eucharist.

✠ Ecumenical dialogue is based on everyone's right and duty to express, with serenity and objectivity, his or her identity, highlighting what each one is, what unites and what divides. Clearly expressing one's positions does not limit ecumenical dialogue, but fosters it.

Why does ecumenism exist?

Because there exist among Christians divisions that are contrary to the will of Christ, who prayed "that they may all be one" (Jn 17:21), so that they might come to the unity of all Christians as "one flock, one shepherd" (Jn 10:16), until "God's People . . . happily arrives at the fullness of eternal glory in the heavenly Jerusalem" (*Unitatis Redintegratio*, no. 3).

Benedict XVI asserts that Christians are now aggravating their divisions in two ways in particular:

- Because of "so-called 'prophetic actions' that are based on a hermeneutic not always consonant with the datum of Scripture and Tradition. Communities consequently give up the attempt to act as a unified body, choosing instead to function according to the idea of 'local options.' Somewhere in this process the need for diachronic *koinonia*—communion with the Church in every age—is lost, just at the time when the world is losing its bearings and needs a persuasive common witness to the saving power of the Gospel."

■ Many Christians maintain that they must "follow his or her own conscience and choose a community that best suits his or her individual tastes. The result is seen in the continual proliferation of communities which often eschew institutional structures and minimize the importance of doctrinal content for Christian living. Even within the ecumenical movement, Christians may be reluctant to assert the role of doctrine for fear that it would only exacerbate rather than heal the wounds of division" (Address, Ecumenical prayer service in New York at St. Joseph's Parish, April 18, 2008).

What kinds of evil do divisions cause among Christians?

✠ They cause various kinds of evil, both within the Church and outside of it. In fact:

■ They are a scandal that weakens the voice of the Gospel.

■ "The divisions among Christians prevent the Church from affecting the fullness of catholicity proper to her in those of her sons who, though joined to her by baptism, are yet separated from full communion with her. Furthermore, the Church herself finds it more difficult to express in actual life her full catholicity in all its aspects" (*Unitatis Redintegratio*, no. 4).

- Christian division "also injures the Catholic Church, called by the Lord to become for all 'one flock' with 'one shepherd,' in that it hinders the complete fulfillment of its universality in history" (Congregation for the Doctrine of the Faith, *Communionis Notio*, no. 17).

✠ This lack of unity among Christians also causes serious damage to the witness that Christians are required to present to non-Christians: it constitutes a counter-witness. "It is sad that in this situation, Christians should lose part of their missionary and evangelizing impulse because of the divisions that undermine their interior life and reduce their apostolic credibility" (Pontifical Council for Christian Unity, *Directory for the Application of Principles and Norms on Ecumenism*, preface).

Why is it necessary to distinguish between the unity of the Church and the unity of Christians?

✠ Because the unity of the Church already exists, "that unity of the one and only Church which Christ bestowed on His Church from the beginning . . . we believe [that this unity] dwells in the Catholic Church as something she can never lose, and we hope that it will continue to increase until the end of time" (*Unitatis Redintegratio*, no. 4). This is why we proclaim in the Creed, "We believe in one . . . Church," and this Church subsists in the Catholic Church (see *Lumen Gentium*, no. 8).

✠ What is lacking is the unity of Christians. In fact, "from her beginnings there arose in this one and only Church of God certain rifts, which the apostle strongly censures as damnable. But in subsequent centuries more widespread dis-agreements appeared and quite large Communities became separated from full communion with the Catholic Church— developments for which, at times, men of both sides were to blame" (*Unitatis Redintegratio*, no. 3).

✠ "The unity of the one Church that already subsists in the Catholic Church and can never be lost is our guarantee that the full unity of all Christians will also one day be a reality" (Pope John Paul II, Homily, November 13, 2004).

✠ And nonetheless the Christians separated from full com-munion with the Catholic Church already have many ele-ments in common with it.

What are the elements that the non-Catholic Christian communities have in common with the Catholic Church?

✠ The members of these non-Catholic Churches and Chris-tian communities

- "Justified by faith through baptism are incorporated into Christ . . . have a right to be honored by the title of Christian, and are properly regarded as brothers in the Lord by the sons of the Catholic Church" (*Unita-tis Redintegratio*, no. 3)
- Have "some, even very many, of the most significant elements or endowments which together go to build up and give life to the Church herself . . . [such as] the written word of God; the life of grace; faith, hope, and charity, along with the other interior gifts of the

Holy Spirit and visible elements" (*Unitatis Redinte-gratio*, no. 3)

✠ "The Spirit of Christ has not refrained from using them as means of salvation which derive their efficacy from the very fullness of grace and truth entrusted to the Catholic Church . . . All of these . . . come from Christ and lead back to Him" (*Unitatio Redintegratio*, no. 3) and "possess an inner dynamism toward catholic unity" (*Lumen Gentium*, no. 8).

✠ "The Church recognizes that in many ways she is linked with those who, being baptized, are honored with the name of Christian, though they do not profess the faith in its entirety or do not preserve unity of communion with the successor of Peter" (*Lumen Gentium*, no. 15).

✠ At the same time, the Catholic Church recognizes that the Orthodox churches are closer to it than the non-Catholic Christian communities are, in that there is no small difference between the two.

What is the difference between the Orthodox Churches and the non-Catholic ecclesial communities?

✠ The Orthodox churches

- "Possess true sacraments, above all—by apostolic succession—the priesthood and the Eucharist, whereby they are still joined to us in a very close relationship" (*Unitatis Redintegratio*, no. 1). Therefore "given suitable circumstances and the approval of Church authority, some worship in common is not merely possible but is recommended." (*Unitatis Redintegratio*, no. 15).

■ Deserve the title of "particular or local Churches," and are called "sister" Churches of the particular Catholic Churches (*Unitatis Redintegratio*, no. 14). Through the celebration of the Eucharist of the Lord in these individual Churches, the Church of God is built up and grows.

■ Have such a profound communion with the Catholic Church "that it lacks little to attain the fullness that would permit a common celebration of the Lord's Eucharist" (Pope Paul VI, Discourse, December 14, 1975)

■ Are not, however, in full communion with the Catholic Church, in that they are not in communion with the visible head of the one Catholic Church who is the pope, the successor of Peter. And this is not a trivial matter, but one of the constitutive internal principles of every particular Church. Therefore, "since communion with the Catholic Church, the visible head of which is the Bishop of Rome and the Successor of Peter, is not some external complement to a particular Church but rather one of its internal constitutive principles, these venerable Christian communities lack something in their condition as particular churches" (CDF, *Responses to Some Questions Regarding Certain Aspects of the Doctrine on the Church* [*Doctrine on the Church*], no. 4).

✠ The non-Catholic ecclesial communities

- Are above all the ones that emerged from the Reformation in the 16th century: Protestant (inspired by the thought and work of Martin Luther, 1483-1546), Anglican (born with the Act of Supremacy of King Henry VIII in 1534) . . . In addition to these, the number of new Christian denominations is constantly multiplying.

- Do not have apostolic succession in the Sacrament of Holy Orders, and thus they are devoid of an essential constitutive element of being Church

- Especially because of the lack of the magisterial priesthood, have not preserved the genuine and complete substance of the Eucharistic mystery (see *Unitatis Redintegratio*, no. 22). "It is for this reason that, for the Catholic Church, Eucharistic intercommunion with these communities is not possible" (CCC, no. 1400).

- "Nevertheless, when they commemorate the Lord's death and resurrection in the Holy Supper, they profess that it signifies life in communion with Christ and they await His coming in glory" (*Unitatis Redintegratio*, no. 22).

- Cannot, according to Catholic doctrine, be called "Churches" in the proper sense (see CDF, *Dominus Iesus*, no. 17), in that they lack the Sacraments of Holy Orders and the Eucharist

In them are found nonetheless "many elements of sanctification and of truth," which "as gifts properly belonging to the Church of Christ, possess an inner dynamism toward Catholic unity" (*Lumen Gentium*, no. 8), such as Sacred Scripture, Baptism, charity . . .

What is the important principle in ecumenical dialogue?

In ecumenical dialogue, "there will always be the principle of fraternal love and the search for mutual understanding and *rapprochement*. Yet we must also be concerned with defending the faith of our people, confirming them in the joyful certitude that "*unica Christi Ecclesia . . . subsistit in Ecclesia catholica, a successore Petri et Episcopis in eius communione gubernata*" ['The one Church of Christ . . . subsists in the Catholic Church which is governed by the successor of Peter and by the Bishops in communion with him'] (*Lumen Gentium*, no. 8)" (Pope Benedict XVI, Address, May 11, 2007).

How must the affirmation that the Church of Christ subsists in the Catholic Church be understood?

"Christ 'established here on earth' only one Church and instituted it as a 'visible and spiritual community,' that from its beginning and throughout the centuries has always existed and will always exist, and in which alone are found all the elements that Christ himself instituted. 'This one Church of Christ, which we confess in the Creed as one, holy, catholic and apostolic [. . .]. This Church, constituted and organized in this world as a society, subsists in the Catholic Church, governed by the successor of Peter and the Bishops in communion with him.'

"In number 8 of the Dogmatic Constitution *Lumen Gentium*, 'subsistence' means this enduring historical continuity and the permanence of all the elements instituted by Christ in the Catholic Church, in which the Church of Christ is concretely found on this earth" (*Doctrine on the Church*, no. 2).

Why does Vatican Council II, in *Lumen Gentium*, use the expression "subsists in," and not the verb "is"?

✠ With the word "subsists," the Council

- Indicates the complete identification of the Church of Christ with the Catholic Church. Since the Church willed by Christ in fact continues to exist (subsist) in the Catholic Church, the continuity of subsistence involves a substantial identity of essence between the Church of Christ and the Catholic Church. The Council therefore wanted to teach that the Church of Jesus Christ as a concrete subject in this world can be found in the Catholic Church.

- Affirms that this word "subsists" "can only be attributed to the Catholic Church alone precisely because it refers to the mark of unity that we profess in the symbols of the faith (I believe . . . in the 'one' Church)" (*Doctrine on the Church*, no. 2)

- Expresses the singular and non-multipliable nature of the Church of Christ. The Church of Christ is only one and subsists, in historical reality, in a single subject, which is the Catholic Church.

- Safeguards the unity and unicity of the Church, which would be lost if one were to admit that there can be multiple subsistences of the Church founded by Christ

- Combats the tendency to imagine the Church of Christ as "'the sum total of the Churches or the ecclesial Communities—which are simultaneously differentiated and yet united,' or 'to think that the Church of Christ no longer exists today concretely and therefore can only be the object of research for the Churches and the communities" (CDF, *Mysterium Ecclesiae*, no. 1). If it were so, the one Church of Christ would no longer exist as "one" in history, or would exist only in an ideal way, evolving toward a future convergence or reunification of the different sister Churches, furthered by dialogue.

- Expresses more clearly how outside of the visible structure of the Catholic Church there are "many elements of sanctification and of truth," which "as gifts properly belonging to the Church of Christ, possess an inner dynamism toward Catholic unity." (*Lumen Gentium*, no. 8). It therefore recognizes the presence, in the non-Catholic Christian communities, of ecclesial elements proper to the Church of Christ. "It follows that these separated Churches and Communities, though we believe they suffer from defects already mentioned, have been by no means deprived of significance and importance in the mystery of salvation. For the Spirit of Christ has not refrained from using them as means of salvation which derive their efficacy from the very fullness of grace and truth entrusted to the Catholic Church" (*Unitatis Redintegratio*, no. 3).

- Allows a greater openness on the part of the Catholic Church to the particular requirement of ecumenism to recognize the truly ecclesial character and dimension of the Christian communities not in full communion with the Catholic Church, because of the *plura elementa sanctificationis et veritatis* ("many elements of sanctification and truth") present in them

✠ The expression "subsists in" therefore harmonizes two doctrinal affirmations: on the one hand, that the Church of Christ, in spite of the divisions among Christians, continues to exist fully only in the Catholic Church; and, on the other hand, the existence of numerous elements of sanctification and truth outside of its visible structure, or in the churches and ecclesial communities that are not yet in full communion with the Catholic Church (see *Doctrine on the Church*, no. 3 and Commentary).

What must be done for Christian unity?

Certain things are required in order to respond adequately to this call:

- A permanent *renewal* of the Church in greater fidelity to her vocation; such renewal is the driving-force of the movement toward unity

- *Conversion of heart* as the faithful "try to live holier lives according to the Gospel"; for it is the unfaithfulness of the members to Christ's gift which causes divisions
- *Prayer in common*, because "change of heart and holiness of life, along with public and private prayer for the unity of Christians, should be regarded as the soul of the whole ecumenical movement, and merits the name 'spiritual ecumenism'"
- *Fraternal knowledge of each other*
- *Ecumenical formation* of the faithful and especially of priests
- *Dialogue* among theologians and meetings among Christians of the different churches and communities
- *Collaboration* among Christians in various areas of service to mankind (CCC, no. 821)

✠ "There is no true ecumenism without inner conversion and the purification of memory, without holiness of life in conformity with the Gospel, and above all, without intense and assiduous prayer that echoes the prayer of Jesus" (Pope John Paul II, Homily, November 13, 2004).

✠ "Union with Christ is also union with all those to whom he gives himself. I cannot possess Christ just for myself; I can belong to him only in union with all those who have become, or who will become, his own. Communion draws me out of myself towards him, and thus also towards unity with all Christians" (Pope Benedict XVI, *Deus Caritas Est*, no. 14).

✠

For more on this topic, see the following pontifical documents:

Vatican Council II, *Lumen Gentium; Unitatis Redintegratio*

Pontifical Council for Christian Unity, *Directory for the Application of Principles and Norms on Ecumenism*, 1993

Catechism of the Catholic Church

Congregation for the Doctrine of the Faith, *Responses to Some Questions Regarding Certain Aspects of the Doctrine on the Church*, June 29, 2007

IX
Non-Christian Religions

Above all, the Catholic Church takes a positive view on non-Christian religions.

On what is this positive view founded?

✠ This positive view is expressed and explained by Vatican Council II as follows:

- Since they have just one origin, God, and just one end, God, the non-Christian religions contain traces of goodness, "whatever truth and grace are to be found among the nations, as a sort of secret presence of God" (*Ad Gentes*, no. 9).
- As expressions of the revelation that God has made through the cosmos and humanity, these religions can in a certain way bring into relationship with God those who profess and practice them with upright and sincere hearts.

- The non-Christian religions also bear witness (in a way that is indeed insufficient and incomplete, but still true) to the presence and action of God, or at least of the sacred, in the world, and God alone knows how great the need for this is now, in an age that tends to erase and eliminate any sign or expression of the divine.

- They are also an expression of humanity's search for an answer to its fundamental questions. As the Council says, people expect from the various religions "answers to those profound mysteries of the human condition which, today even as in olden times, deeply stir the human heart: What is a man? What is the meaning and the purpose of our life? What is goodness and what is sin? What gives rise to our sorrows and to what intent? Where lies the path to true happiness? What is the truth about death, judgment, and retribution beyond the grave? What, finally, is that ultimate and unutterable mystery which engulfs our being, and whence we take our rise, and whither our journey leads us?" (*Nostra Aetate*, no. 1).

- The Catholic Church therefore recognizes that in the non-Christian religions there exist "goodness and truth" (*Optatam Totius*, no. 16), "precious elements of religion and humanity" (*Gaudium et Spes*, no. 92), "seeds of the Word" (*Ad Gentes*, no. 11), "a ray of that Truth which enlightens all men" (*Nostra Aetate*, no. 2). "Whatever the Spirit brings about in human hearts and in the history of peoples, in cultures and religions serves as a preparation for the Gospel" (*Redemptoris Missio*, no. 29).

■ If it is true that the Holy Spirit realizes salvation in non-Christians in part through those elements of truth and goodness that are present in the various religions, it is also true that those who do not currently belong to the visible Church are also objectively "oriented" toward it, they are part of that wider Church which is known only to God.

✠ The non-Christian religions therefore deserve the attention and respect of Christians, and their spiritual heritage is an efficacious invitation to dialogue not only on points of similarity, but also on those of difference. Every religion, in fact, has its specificity and originality, which must not be forgotten or disregarded.

What are the main positive characteristics that are common to the various religions?

✠ The religions are expressions of human cultures and preserve their spiritual riches.

✠ They have transmitted and continue to transmit treasures of wisdom and devotion and so have been able to support the human and spiritual journey of many generations.

✠ Through them, everyone has had the opportunity to establish a relationship with God, with the Transcendent, to find resources for moral effort and nourish hope in the afterlife.

✠ In the religions is realized and developed that natural desire to see God that is common to all human beings and constitutes the foundation of every religious attitude. This is a truth that Catholic theology has always affirmed and that St. Thomas Aquinas presented very well in the first pages of the *Summa Theologica*.

✠ "Religions can and must offer precious resources to build a peaceful humanity because they speak of peace to the human heart" (Pope Benedict XVI, Greeting to Christian delegations in Naples, October 21, 2007).

✠ The Catholic Church does not say that all of the religions are on the same level and are more or less the same thing but maintains that all who are seeking God have the same dignity and the same freedom. And this not because their religion is true or false but simply because they are human persons.

✠ "Religious freedom that enables each one to live his belief alone or with others, in private or in public, also requires the possibility for the person to change his religion should his conscience so require" (Pope Benedict XVI, Address, December 18, 2008).

Does the Catholic Church also see negative aspects in non-Christian religions?

✠ It must not be forgotten or ignored, however, that the non-Christian religions also contain false elements, theoretical and practical errors, malformations, deformations, distortions, reductive visions . . .

"In their religious behavior . . . men also display the limits and errors that disfigure the image of God in them" (CCC, no. 844). "Often men, deceived by the Evil One, have become caught up in their futile reasoning and have exchanged the truth of God for a lie, serving the creature rather than the Creator. Or some there are who, living and dying in a world without God, are subject to utter hopelessness" (*Lumen Gentium*, no. 16).

✠ Therefore, "to hold that these religions, considered as such, are ways of salvation, has no foundation in Catholic theology, also because they contain omissions, insufficiencies and errors regarding fundamental truths about God, man and the world" (CDF, *Notification on the Book* Toward a Christian Theology of Religious Pluralism *by Father Jacques Dupuis, SJ* [*Notification*], no. 8).

What are the causes of these negative aspects?

✠ These negative aspects present in non-Christian religions do not depend only or even mainly on the way in which these religions are professed or embodied by different persons or different peoples, in the various times and cultures. This also happens in the Christian faith.

✠ Instead, these negative aspects, these inauthentic elements, are due in large part to the very nature of the non-Christian religions.

In fact, these religions (with the exception of the Jewish religion) are for the most part the fruit and effect of efforts and attempts made by human beings to reach God and to come into contact with him, although this does not rule out the possibility that in some cases the founders of these religions may have received some particular gift from above.

✠ Now, precisely because of their human origin, it is normal for them to contain deformed, erroneous, incomplete elements, very often due to the fact that the divinities reflect human beings, they are made in the image and likeness of human limitations and defects. The history of the religions attests that in many cases human beings have imagined and made divinities in their own image and likeness. On the contrary, the Bible, right from the book of Genesis, reminds us that it is God who made human beings in his own image and likeness and who calls human beings to share in his life, giving them the capacity and power to realize this objective.

✠ The risk of producing and accumulating these negative aspects is even greater if one considers that human beings are sinners and live under the influence of personal and collective sin and of the "principle of evil": the Devil.

✠ Because of these negative aspects, "one must not automatically see in all religions ways of God toward human beings and of human beings toward God" (Cardinal Ratzinger, *Fede, Verità, Tolleranza*, 78).

What does the Catholic Church do with regard to the positive and negative present in non-Christian religions?

✠ The Catholic Church

- Respects and "assumes" all that is good and positive in the different religions
- At the same time, in the light of the Gospel, identifies, purifies, and frees from contamination and from spurious elements that which is assumed, candidly condemning anything that is ignoble, dehumanizing, or contrary to the Gospel in it
- Cultivates a serene and sincere dialogue with all religions, not only on what unites them, but also on the differences. "In our attempt to discover points of commonality, perhaps we have shied away from the responsibility to discuss our differences with calmness and clarity . . . The higher goal of interreligious dialogue requires a clear exposition of our respective religious tenets" (Pope Benedict XVI, Meeting with representatives of other religions, Washington, DC, April 18, 2008). True interreligious dialogue, therefore, involves
  - Not being interested only in the points in common
  - Presenting the respective differences, and this not for the sake of mutual opposition, but for the healthy growth of all
  - Not only proclaiming the truth, but also condemning errors

- Affirming the absolute novelty and originality of the Christian faith, which consists in the fact that in Christianity it is not human beings who approach God, but it is God who draws near to human beings and who above all becomes human in Jesus Christ, who, precisely through his Death on the Cross and his Resurrection, wants to save all human beings, giving them the Holy Spirit, who makes them children of God.

✠ In this sense, the Christian faith does not say that human beings reconcile themselves with God, but that "God was reconciling the world to himself in Christ" (2 Cor 5:19).

It is therefore legitimate to maintain that the Holy Spirit achieves the salvation of non-Christians in part through those elements of truth and goodness that are present in the various religions. But it is completely false and contrary to Catholic doctrine "to hold that these religions, considered as such, are ways of salvation . . . also because they contain omissions, insufficiencies and errors regarding fundamental truths about God, man and the world" (*Notification*, no. 8).

What should be done to foster interreligious dialogue among the various religions?

✠ There are various and complementary initiatives that can be undertaken in this regard (from the Pontifical Council for Interreligious Dialogue, *Christians and Muslims: Together in Overcoming Violence Among Followers of Different Religions*, August 27, 2010):

- To open our hearts to mutual forgiveness and reconciliation, for a peaceful and fruitful coexistence
- To recognize what we have in common and to respect differences, as a basis for a culture of dialogue
- To recognize and respect the dignity and the rights of each human being without any bias related to ethnicity or religious affiliation
- Necessity to promulgate just laws which guarantee the fundamental equality of all
- To recall the importance of education towards respect, dialogue and fraternity in the various educational arenas: at home, in the school, in churches and mosques.

   Thus we will be able to oppose violence among followers of different religions and promote peace and harmony among the various religious communities.

✠ "Teaching by religious leaders, as well as school books which present religions in an objective way, have, along with teaching in general, a decisive impact on the education and the formation of younger generations."

How could the points presented above be summarized?

Regarding the non-Christian religions and the religious traditions in general:

✠ What do they express?

- The restlessness of the human heart

- The yearning for the Absolute
- The answer to the great questions of existence

✠ What relationship do they have with Christianity?

- They are ways leading toward the Truth.
- They contain the *semina Verbi* (seeds of the Word of God: Jesus Christ).

✠ They are surrounded

- By the mysterious paternity of God the Father in relation to all
- By the universal efficacy of Christ, the sole and definitive Savior
- By the active presence of the Holy Spirit, who fills all things and everyone

✠ Their positive religious aspects

- Come from God
- Are gifts from Christ, glimmers and reflections of his truth
- Are part of what the Spirit does in human hearts and in the history of the peoples, in cultures and religions
- Can take on a role of preparation for the Gospel, as occasions for learning in which human hearts are stimulated to open themselves to the action of God

✠ Because of this, these positive aspects present in the other religions demand on the part of Christians

- ■ Recognition
- ■ Respect
- ■ Appreciation

✠ Nonetheless, these positive aspects are

- ■ Awaiting purification/fulfillment/completeness in Christ
- ■ In an objectively deficient situation
- ■ Mixed with negative aspects
- ■ Not effective *ex opere operato* (the action, the sign, does not in and of itself bring about what it signifies)

What are the main characteristics of the Catholic Church?

✠ The Catholic Church

- ■ Proclaims and communicates Christ, who is the one Savior of all
- ■ Affirms that
  - "Christ 'established here on earth' only one Church and instituted it as a 'visible and spiritual community,' that from its beginning and throughout the centuries has always existed and will always exist, and in which alone are found all the elements that Christ himself instituted. 'This one Church of Christ, which we confess in the Creed as one, holy, catholic and apostolic [. . .]. This Church, constituted and organized in this world as a society, subsists in the Catholic Church, governed by the successor of Peter and

the Bishops in communion with him.' In number 8 of the Dogmatic Constitution *Lumen Gentium* 'subsistence' means this enduring, historical continuity and the permanence of all the elements instituted by Christ in the Catholic Church, in which the Church of Christ is concretely found on this earth.

- "The Church of Christ is present and operative in the churches and ecclesial Communities not yet fully in communion with the Catholic Church, on account of the elements of sanctification and truth that are present in them.

- "Nevertheless, the word 'subsists' can only be attributed to the Catholic Church alone precisely because it refers to the mark of unity that we profess in the symbols of the faith (I believe . . . in the 'one' Church); and this 'one' Church subsists in the Catholic Church" (*Doctrine on the Church*, no. 2).

- The ecclesial communities that "because of the lack of the sacrament of orders . . . have not preserved the genuine and total reality of the Eucharistic mystery" (*Unitatis Redintegratio*, no. 22) cannot be called "Churches" in the proper sense

- Offers to human beings of every time, age, culture, nationality, etc., the possibility to realize fully and authentically that fullness of truth and happiness for which they ceaselessly strive

- Is the sign and instrument of salvation for all people. "It must be firmly believed that 'the Church, a pilgrim now on earth, is necessary for salvation: the one Christ is the mediator and the way of salvation; he is present to us in his body which is the Church' (*Lumen Gentium*, no. 20)" (*Dominus Iesus*, no. 20). The Church is the "universal sacrament of salvation" (*Lumen Gentium*, no. 48). Therefore the followers of other religions are also ordered to the Catholic Church, and all of them are called to become part of it, in that outside of its visible structure there are "many elements of sanctification and of truth," which "as gifts properly belonging to the Church of Christ, possess and inner dynamism toward Catholic unity." (*Lumen Gentium*, no. 8).

✠ The Christian faith therefore has within itself, objectively, "something more" with respect to the other religions (although unfortunately Christians do not always reflect, in their thoughts and actions, this "something more," thereby justifying the statement, "I admire Christianity, but not Christians").

✠ Because of this, the Christian religion cannot be put on the same level as the other religions, to the point that "one religion is as good as another." This would also constitute an offense to what is specific and different in the various religions, and above all would be a grave offense to Jesus Christ, rendering useless

- The will of God, his Father and ours, who "wills everyone to be saved and to come to knowledge of the truth" (1 Tm 2:4)
- His coming among us, realized so that "they might have life and have it more abundantly" (Jn 10:10)
- His Death and Resurrection, which have universal salvific efficacy
- His commandment, "Go into the whole world and proclaim the gospel to every creature. Whoever believes and is baptized will be saved; whoever does not believe will be condemned" (Mk 16: 15-16).

How are the members of non-Christian religions saved?

"Those also can attain to everlasting salvation who through no fault of their own do not know the gospel of Christ or His Church, yet sincerely seek God and, moved by grace, strive by their deeds to do His will as it is known to them through the dictates of conscience" (*Lumen Gentium*, no. 16).

For those who are saved, does their salvation always come from Christ and through his Church?

Certainly, even if they do not realize it. In fact, all salvation comes from Christ the Head, the only Savior, through the Church that is his Body. It is therefore the Church's duty to proclaim to the whole world that Jesus Christ is the only Savior of all.

Why is Jesus Christ the only Savior?

✠ Because:

- By the will of God the Father, "there is no salvation through anyone else, nor is there any other name under heaven given to the human race by which we are to be saved" (Acts 4:12).
- No one can know or enter into communion with the Triune God except through Jesus Christ (see Jn 16:6).
- God has spoken and given all that he is in his Only-Begotten Son, Jesus Christ. So no new revelation or gift is to be expected: this would be an offense against Christ.
- Christ is the full and definitive Revealer of the Father and Savior of humanity. He is the Mediator and the only Way of salvation.
- He is the One who, as the Only-Begotten Son of God the Father, can satisfy the hunger and thirst for Truth and Happiness in the human heart.

✠ Jesus Christ is the "splendor of the glory" of the one God and Father. He is the Son, in the full sense, of God the Father, and is therefore the One who allows us to know God perfectly, making him present in the midst of humanity. He is Light and Life, as St. John proclaims in the prologue of his Gospel: "Through him was life, and this life was the light of the human race" (Jn 1:4).